A DICTIONARY OF GRAPHICAL SYMBOLS

A DICTIONARY OF Graphical Symbols

L. J. Robinson

F. C. Avis
London

Made and printed in England

F. C. Avis
26 Gordonbrock Road, London, S.E.4

211.26840.2

MANY HUNDREDS OF GRAPHICAL SYMBOLS are in common use, and thousands more appear as conventional or specialized signs in publications concerned with science, mathematics, travel, technology, music, etc. Type design and letter forms have additional significance and a peculiar nomenclature.

A

A: the first letter of the alphabet.

Aa Aa Aa Aa

Abnormal Visibility: see Air, pure.

A to Z Length: the length of the lower-case alphabet, used to determine whether a type is normal, wide or narrow, the standard length being 13 ems of the particular type body.

abcdefghijklmnopqrstuvwxyz

abcdefghijklmnopqrstuvwxyz

abcdefghijklmnopqrstuvwxyz

Accents: see under the names of the individual accents, Accents, floating, and also under the respective languages.

Accents, Floating: those cast on a body independent of that of the letters with which they are used; also known as loose accents.

ˇ ˆ ´ ` ¯ ˜ ˘ ʿ ¨ ˝ ˚ ʾ ˙ over letter

¸ ʾ ˛ . under letter

Account: a commercial symbol, abbreviation for the word account.

a/c a/c a/c a/c a/c a/c a/c a/c a/c a/c a/c

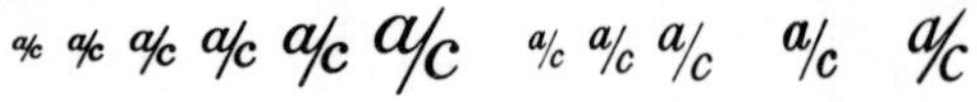

Accumbent: see Cotyledon.

Actinium: a radio-active element. (Ac) 

Actor: a symbol used to indicate actor in directories, in which composition space and time must be saved; the same symbol used for Drama.

Acute Accent: may be used on any of the vowels, and certain of the consonants; slopes up from left to right.

á é í ó ú ć ń ŕ ś ý ź

Acute Angles: mathematical symbols of various significance; see also Right Angle.

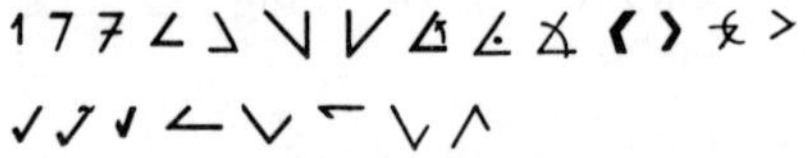

Addition: a symbol used to join two or more numbers into one sum; also known as plus.

\+ + + + + + +

\+ + + + + +

\+ + + + + +

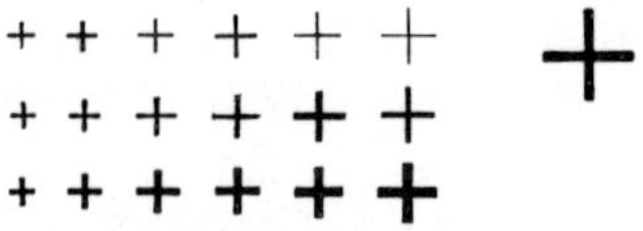

Admiration, Note of: see Exclamation.

Æ: see Diphthong.

Aeroplane: a sign used, particularly in timetables, to indicate aerial connection.

Agriculturalist: a symbol used to indicate land worker in directories, in which composition space and time must be saved.

Air, Pure: a meteorological symbol, also referred to as Abnormal visibility.

0

Albanian Accents: the circumflex, cedilla and diæresis are used.

âçë ÂÇË

Aleph: see Hebrew alphabet.

Alignment: uniform ranging of letters at the foot.

Base Line...... Alignment ....

Almanack Signs: stylized abbreviations for the names of days of the week.

S M Tu W Th F S

Alpha: see Greek alphabet.

Alphabet: the letters arranged in order; in English, consists of 26 letters and two diphthongs; a book fount contains three alphabets, capitals, small capitals and lower-case; a display fount usually two, capitals and lower-case.

ABCDEFGHIJKLMNOPQRSTUVWXYZÆŒ
ABCDEFGHIJKLMNOPQRSTUVWXYZÆŒ
abcdefghijklmnopqrstuvwxyzæœ

Alphabet: CONTINUED

ABCDEFGHIJKL
MNOPQRSTUVW
XYZÆŒ
abcdefghijklmno
pqrstuvwxyzæœ

Alternation: a symbol used in electricity and magnetism.

~

Alternative Characters: letters, etc., of distinctive design, intended for special use.

a e k r s u z E K S CJKQR *ANV*
a e k r s u z E K S CJKQR *ANV*

A K M N R W efp *M* S
A K M N R W efp *M* S

1234567890 V W
1234567890 V W

A E K M N W E R *C E F*
A E K M N W E R *C E F*

QR **EM** RY **MW**
QR **EM** RY **MW**

Aluminium: the metallic base of alumina. (Al)

Americium: a transuranic radio-active element. (Am)

Ampersand: the abbreviated form of the word and; also known as am pussy and, curly and, round and, short and.

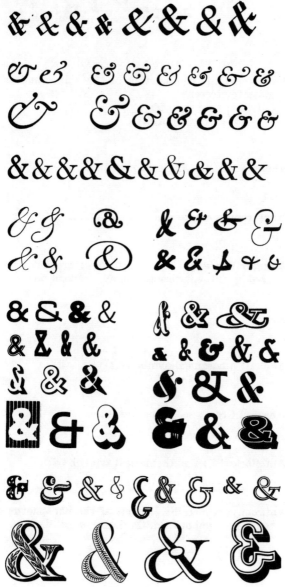

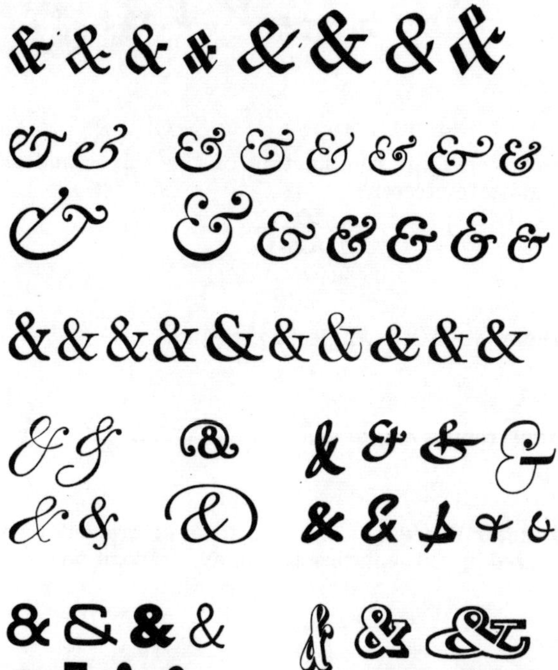

Am Pussy And: see Ampersand.

Anchor: a nautical symbol or ornament.

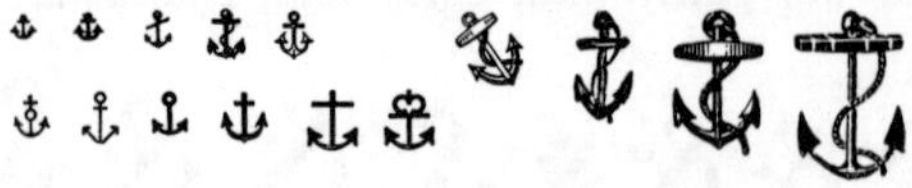

Andcetera: the combination of the ampersand and c to indicate etcetera.

&c

Angle: see Acute Angle, Right Angle.

Angstrom: a unit of electrical measurement. Å

Angular Bracket: a stylized form of bracket (sometimes used in mathematics or display composition).

⟨ ⟩

Annual: a botanical symbol. ①

Ansated Cross: see Crux Ansata.

Anticlockwise: a mathematical symbol. ↺

Antimony: a metallic element of the phosphorus group; takes its symbol from the Latin word Stibium.

Ⓢⓑ (Sb)

Antiqua: the German name for types of roman design.

Diethelm-Antiqua Schadow Antiqua

Antique: a medium weight type face, with rather prominent old style or slab serifs, akin to Clarendon and Egyptian.

ANTIQUE No 3

OLD STYLE ANTIQUE

Anvil: see Blacksmith.

Apex: the highest point of a letter, especially at the junction of two strokes.

Apostrophe: a punctuation mark denoting omission or possession, or to end a quotation, standing high on the shoulder.

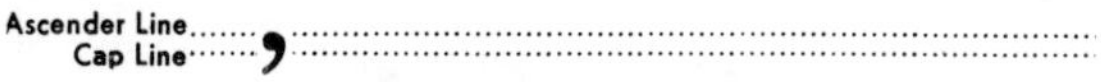

Apothecary: a symbol used to indicate chemist or druggist in directories, in which composition space and time must be saved.

Approaches: a mathematical symbol. $\rightarrow$

Approximately Equal: a mathematical symbol.

$\fallingdotseq \quad \doteqdot \quad \approx \quad \simeq \quad \bumpeq$

Aquarius: see Zodiac, Signs of.

Arabic Figures: those comprising the numerals 1 to 0.

1234567890

1234567890

1234567890

1234567890

Arbor: a botanical sign for a tree (exceeding 25 ft. high).

Arbuscula: a botanical sign for a small tree or shrub.

Arc: a geometrical symbol, part of the circumference of a circle or other curve.

Archæological Signs: graphical signs, particularly combined letters, used in ancient carvings, etc.

Archæologist: a symbol used to indicate archæologist in directories, in which composition space and time must be saved.

Archbishop's Cross: see Patriarchal cross.

Architect: a symbol used to indicate architect in directories, in which composition space and time must be saved.

Arc of Stem: the curved portion of a stem in letters such as lower-case m.

m n u

Argon: an element contained in the atmosphere. Ⓐ

Aries: see Zodiac, Signs of.

Arm: a horizontal or diagonal line of a letter.

E F K L T Z

Arroba: a Spanish and Portuguese measure of weight, about 25 lb.

@

Arrow: the symbol of this name; see also Broad Arrow.

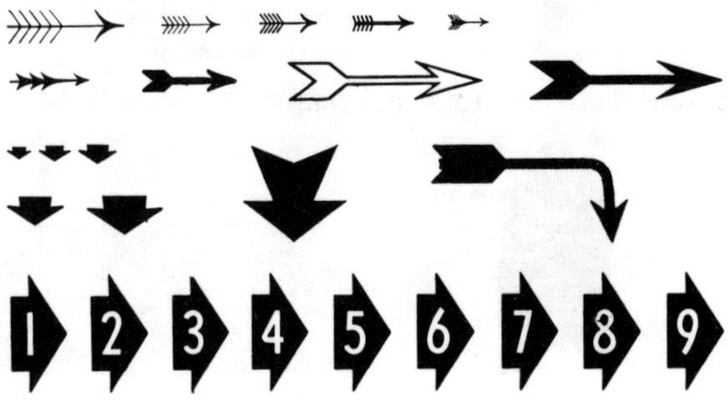

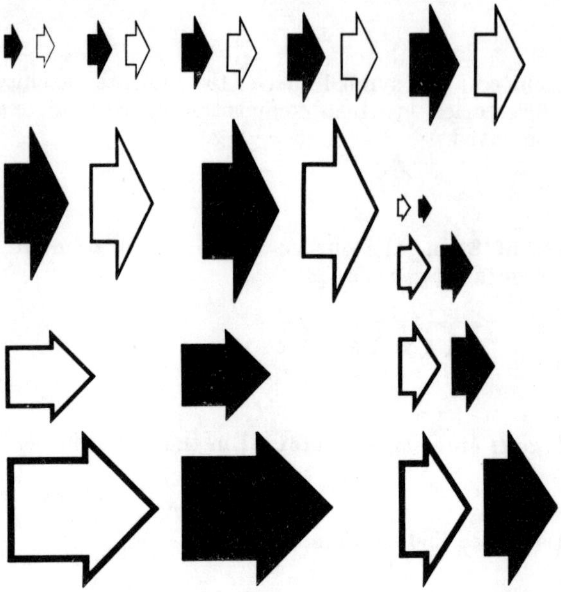

Arrow Head: the barbed, forward part of the arrow.

Arrow Shaft: that portion of an arrow between head and tail.

Arrow Tail: the terminal portion of an arrow.

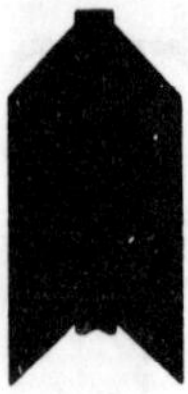

Arsenic: a poisonous semi-metallic element. (As)

Ascender: a lower-case letter with ascending stroke or the ascending stroke itself; the term also sometimes applied to capital letters.

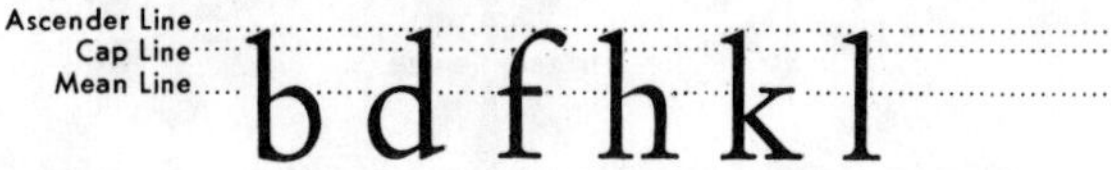

Ascender Line: the imaginary line to which ascending letters normally reach.

Asper: see Breathings.

Assertion: a mathematical symbol. ⊢

Astatine: a radio-active element. (At)

Asterisk: the first bookwork reference mark (usually distinguished from the Star, q.v.); also used to denote an omitted letter in a word.

Asterisk: CONTINUED

Asterism: a triangular group of asterisks.

⁂

Asteroid: a small planet between the orbits of Mars and Jupiter; the principal asteroids are:

Astræa	Hebe	Pallas ⚴ or ⚴
Ceres ⚳ or ⚳	Iris	Vesta ⚶
Flora	Juno ⚵	

Astræa: see Asteroid.

Astronomer: a symbol used to indicate astronomer in directories, in which composition space and time must be saved.

Astronomical Signs: see under individual names (Sun, Uranus, etc.).

At: see Commercial a.

Augmented Roman Alphabet: see Pitman's Augmented Alphabet.

Aurora: a meteorological symbol. 

Author: a symbol used to indicate author in directories, in which composition space and time must be saved.

Automobile: a conventional sign, often used in timetables to indicate correspondence with rail or other services.

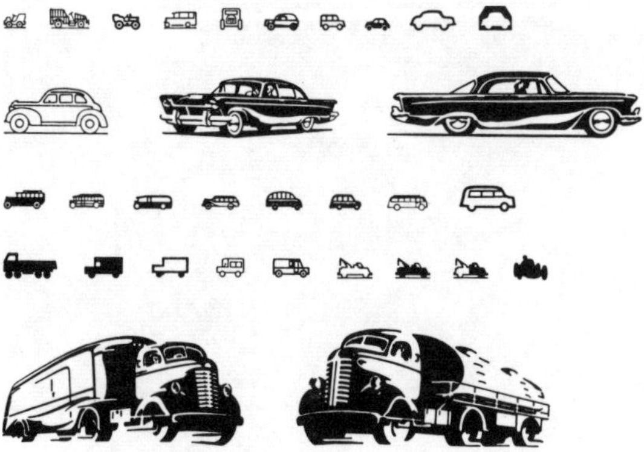

B

B: the second letter of the English alphabet.

Bb Bb Bb Bb

Background: decoration or patterns serving to throw up the actual type character; see also Initial Letters.

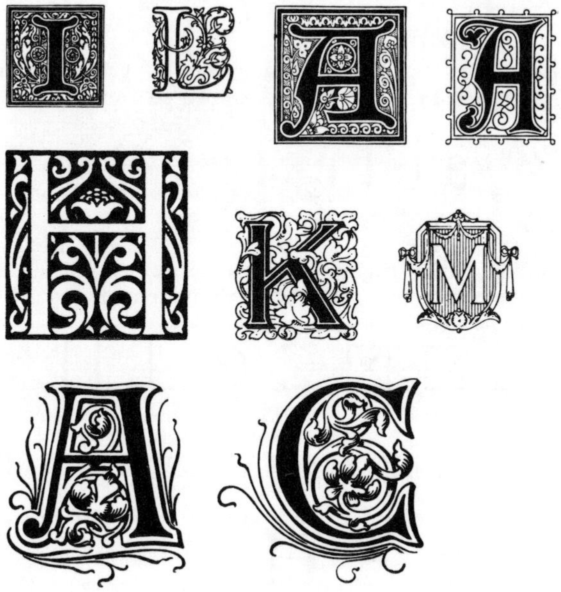

Background: CONTINUED

Backhand: a type face sloping up from right to left.

Pen Print   Backslant

Ball: the terminal at the end of certain strokes in Modern type faces; also known as Dot.

a c f i j J r y

Ballot Paper Signs: squares or circles, either blank or enclosing cross, as used on voting papers.

Bar[1]**:** a horizontal connecting line between two strokes of a letter.

e A H

Bar[2]**:** a light perpendicular line.

Bar[3]**:** a division of the musical stave, indicated by a perpendicular line.

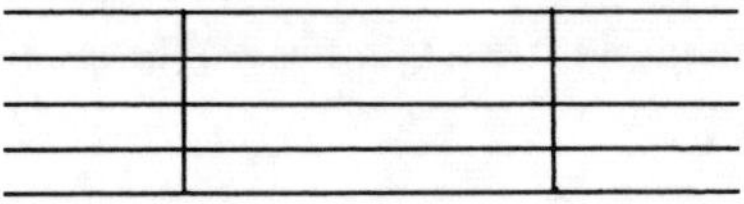

Barb[1]**:** the arrowhead. 

Barb[2]**:** see Cat's ear.

Barium: the metallic base of Baryta. (Ba)

Baroque: irregular wavy rule.

Barred C[1]**:** a stylized symbol for cent (a unit of currency).

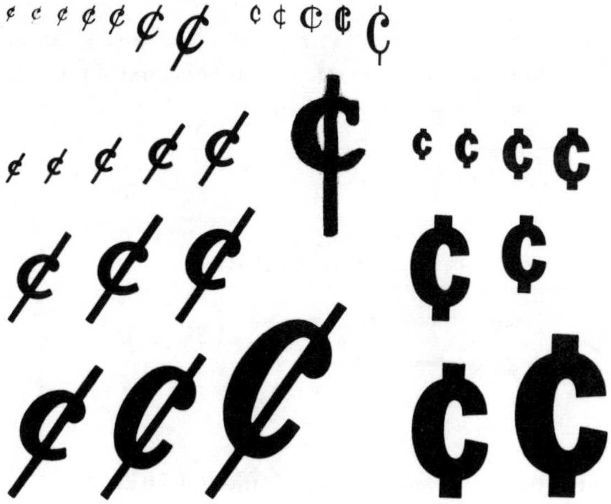

Barred C[1]**:** CONTINUED

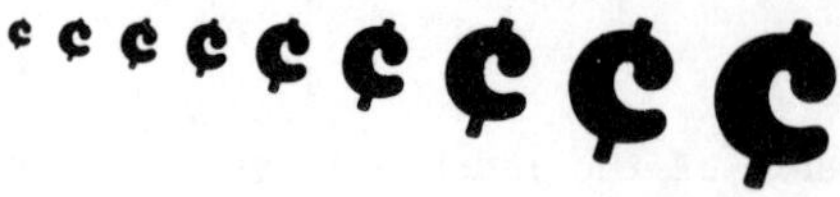

Barred C[2]**:** a time signature (alla breve) in music.

Base Line: the imaginary line upon which most letters stand.

Base Line..... Base Line

Battle: the symbol used on a map to indicate the place where a battle was fought.

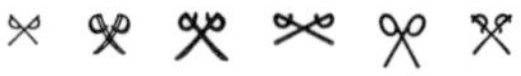

Beak: a serif formed on the arms of a letter.

E F K L T Z

Because: the mathematical symbol used as a contraction for the word because.

∵

Bed: a conventional sign, often used in guide books to indicate sleeping accommodation.

Berkelium: a radio-active element. (Bk)

Beryllium: an earth metal. (Be)

Beta: see Greek alphabet.

Beth: see Hebrew alphabet.

Between: a mathematical symbol. ≬

Bias: see Modelling.

Biennial: a botanical symbol. ②

Bind: a symbol used in music over two or more notes to indicate that they are to be played as one; also known as tie.

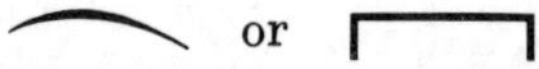

Birth: see Naissance.

Bishop: see Chess.

Bismuth: a metallic element. (Bi)

Black: a very thick design of type face.

Cooper Black

Stymie Black

Tempo Black

Black Dot: see Dot[2].

Black Letter: the design used by the earliest printers; rather heavy, angular and stiff letter forms; also known as Church Text, Old English, or Text.

Tudor Black

Old English Text

Festival Text

Trojan Text

Jessen

Sachsenwald

Wallau

Black Note: a completely filled in note in music. 

Blacksmith: the conventional anvil indicates this trader.

Blind P: see Paragraph.

Block Letter: see Sanserif.

Block Serif: see Slab serif.

Body Types: see Book letters.

Bohemian Accents: see Czech accents.

Bold: a type face thicker than standard.

Craw Modern Bold

Fortune Bold

Goudy Bold

MICROGRAMMA BOLD

Optima Bold

Record Gothic Bold

STUDIO BOLD

Virtuosa Bold

Bolivar: a symbol used in Bolivian currency. Ƀ

Bond[1]**:** a line, either straight or at angle, that ties parts of a chemical formula.

/ — | // = ||

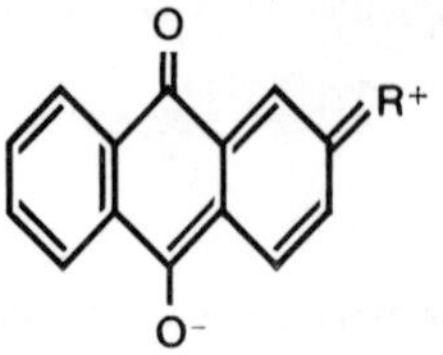

Bond[2]**:** see Vinculum.

Book Letters: those used primarily for bookwork; contain capitals, small capitals and lower-case letters, in addition to a numerous selection of unusual sorts (accents, etc.); must be eminently legible, of medium weight, rather close set, with no ornamentation, and with fairly long ascenders and descenders; also known as body founts. Typical book letters:

ABCDEFGHIJKLMNOPQRSTUVWX

YZÆŒ& RY QU Qu

ABCDEFGHIJKLMNOPQRSTUVWXYZÆŒ QU

abcdefghijklmnopqrstuvwxyzæœfiffflffiffl ßctst

ABCDEFGHIJKLMNOPQRSTUVWXY

ZÆŒ& QU

abcdefghijklmnopqrstuvwxyzæœfiffflffiffl ßctstgg Qu

£1234567890 *£1234567890*

.,:;'"!¡?¿()[]«»/‡†§*¶.–..—... *.,':;"!¡?¿()[]§†*

ÀÁÄÈÉËÊÌÍÒÓÖÙÚÜÑÇ

ÀÁÄÈÉËÊÌÍÒÓÖÙÚÜÑÇ

àáäâèéëêìíïîòóöôùúüûñç

ÀÁÄÈÉËÊÌÍÒÓÖÙÚÜÑÇ

àáäâèéëêìíïîòóöôùúüûñç Poliphilus

Baskerville

ABCDEFGHIJKLMNOPQRSTUVWX
abcdefghijklmnopqrstuvwxyz YZ

Bembo

ABCDEFGHIJKLMNOPQRSTUVWXY
abcdefghijklmnopqrstuvwxyz Z

Caslon Old Face

ABCDEFGHIJKLMNOPQRSTUVWX
abcdefghijklmnopqrstuvwxyz YZ

Dante

ABCDEFGHIJKLMNOPQRSTUVWXYZ
abcdefghijklmnopqrstuvwxyz

Ehrhardt

ABCDEFGHIJKLMNOPQRSTUVWXYZ
abcdefghijklmnopqrstuvwxyz

Plantin

ABCDEFGHIJKLMNOPQRSTUVWX
abcdefghijklmnopqrstuvwxyz YZ

Scotch Roman

ABCDEFGHIJKLMNOPQRSTUVWX
abcdefghijklmnopqrstuvwxyz YZ

Spectrum

ABCDEFGHIJKLMNOPQRSTUVWXY
abcdefghijklmnopqrstuvwxyz Z

Times New Roman

ABCDEFGHIJKLMNOPQRSTUVWX
abcdefghijklmnopqrstuvwxyz YZ

Border: printing element(s) of plain or figured design, as separate units or continuous strips, in brass, type metal, wood, etc., used to surround type matter, etc.

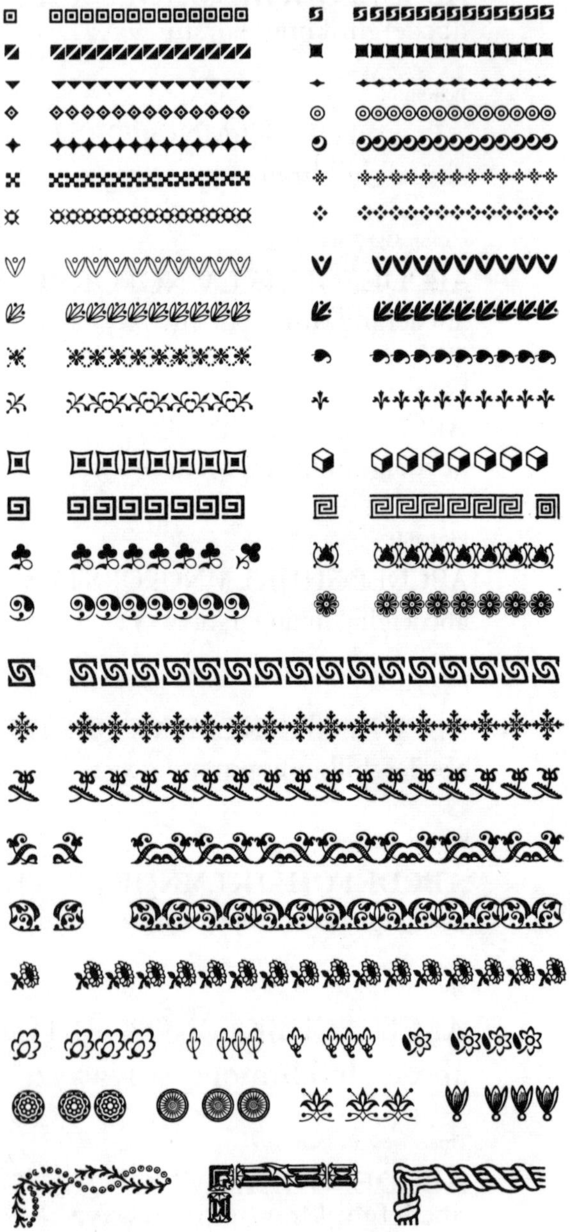

Border: CONTINUED

Border: CONTINUED

Born: see Naissance.

Boron: the main constituent of borax. (B)

Botanical Signs: see under individual names, e.g. Arbor, Cotyledon, etc.

Botanist: a symbol used to indicate botanist in directories, in which composition time and space must be saved.

Bound Letters: see Ligatures.

Bowl: the round part of letters like b, d, etc.

b d p q

Box: a rectangular compartment made up of rule, usually for the surrounding of type matter.

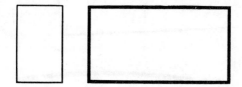

Boxed Figures: those enclosed in a rectangular border, especially as used in calendars.

Box Rules: stylized border shapes in separate and varied pieces, capable of assembly to give widely diverse graphic effects.

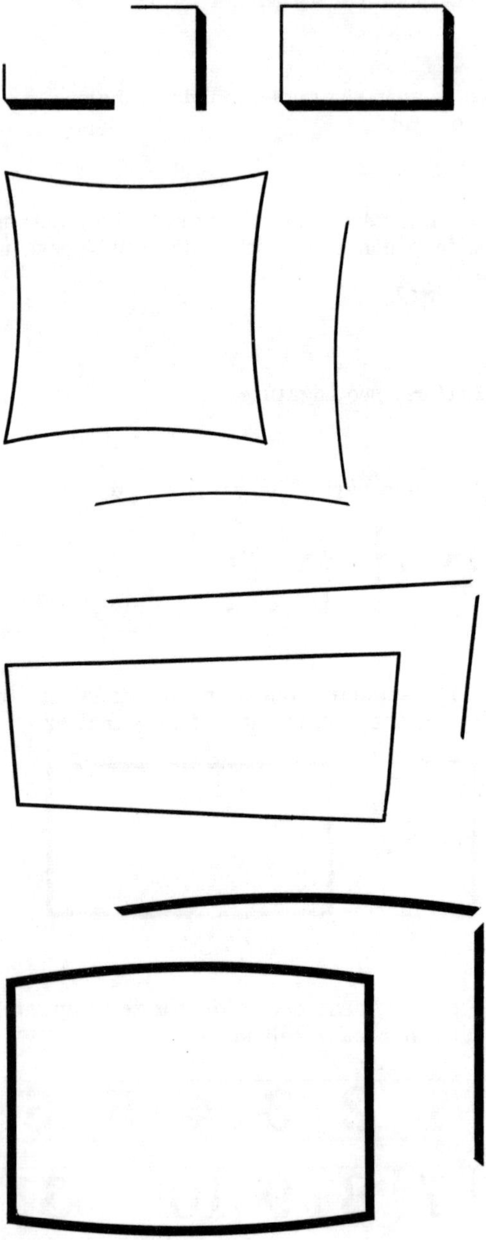

Box Rules: CONTINUED

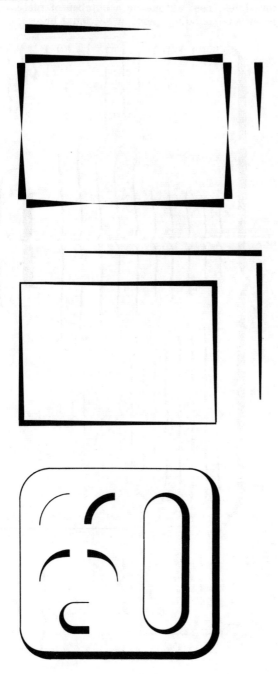

Brace[1]: a double-armed symbol used to connect two or more lines; cast as one or a number of pieces (then known as expanding, piece or sectional brace).

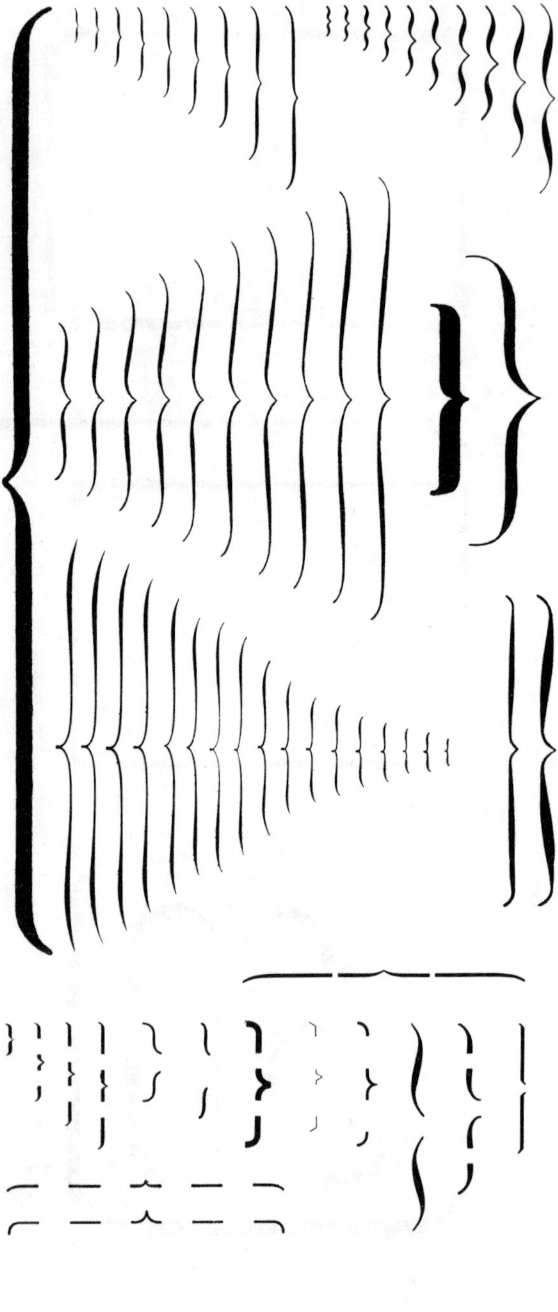

Brace²: see Vinculum.

Bracket¹: a punctuation point used to enclose or cut off words; made as one piece or as a number of pieces. Also known as Crotch, Crotchet. (See also Display bracket.)

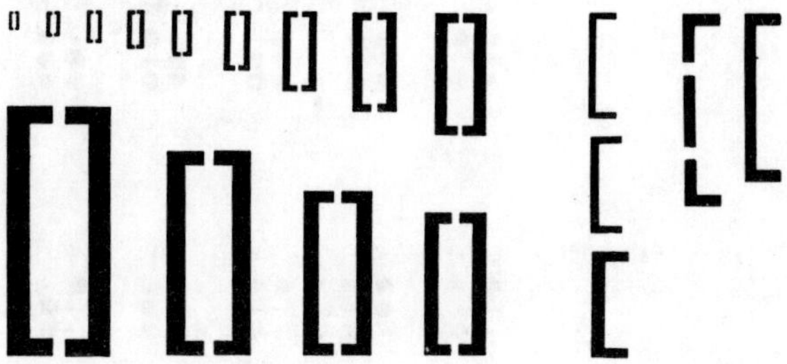

Bracket²: the connecting or hooked piece between serif and stem; also known as fillet or radius.

Braille: type used to print in relief a dotted code for reading by the blind, the heavy dots here representing the raised portions.

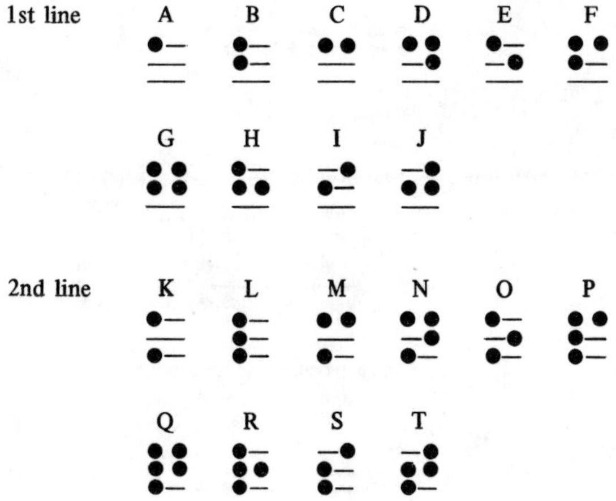

Braille: CONTINUED

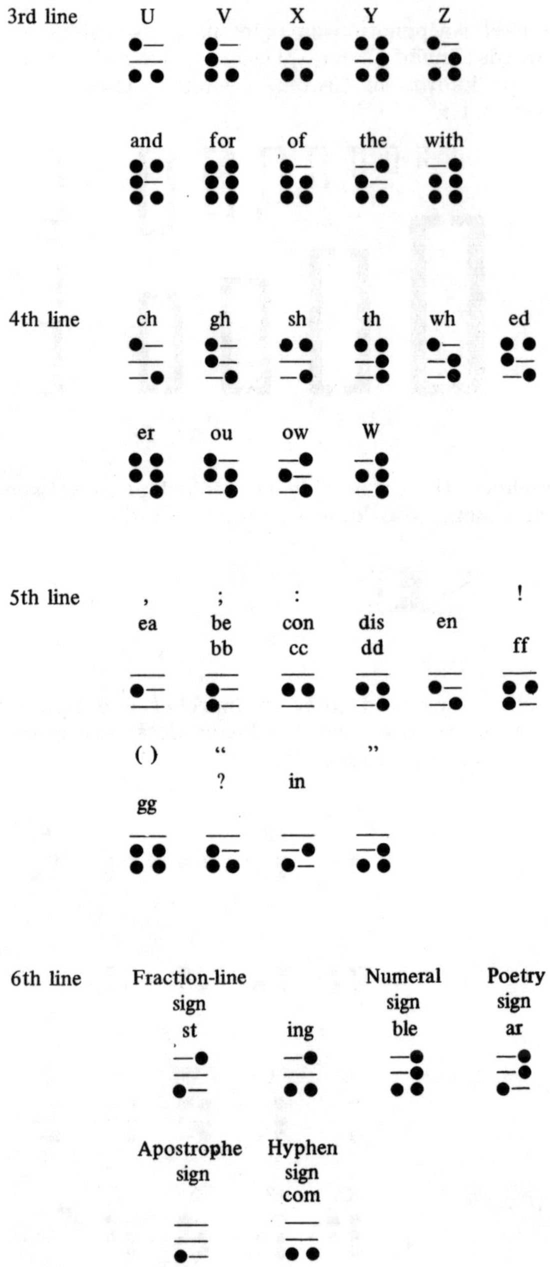

Braille: CONTINUED

7th line — Accent sign

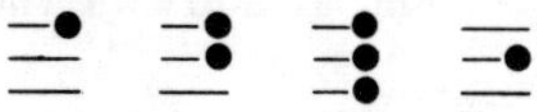

Italic or Decimal-point sign — Letter sign — Capital sign

Used in forming Contractions:

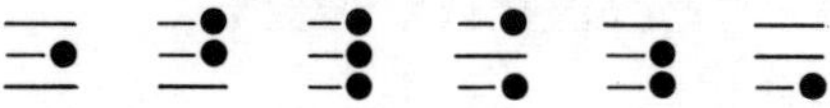

Compound signs — Asterisk * — Dash — Square Brackets [ ]

Inner Inverted Commas ‘ ’

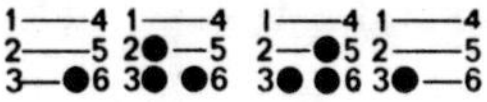

Breath: symbols used in vocal music to denote places where breath should be taken.

Breathings: Greek accents used to denote aspiration or non-aspiration of vowels:

‘ asper (rough) ’ lenis (soft)

Breve[1]**:** the longest musical note now used. 

Breve[2]**:** see Short accent.

Broad Arrow: the official mark of the British Government.

Broad Face: a type considerably wider than standard.

abcdefghijklmno
pqrstuvwxyz

ABCDEFGHIJKL
MNOPQRSTUVWXYZ

Broad Letters: see Hebrew alphabet; Selfspacing type.

Bromine: a non-metallic element. (Br)

Bronze: an alloy of copper and tin. Old symbol (Ch)

Brooklyn Border: one composed of alternate elements of laurel leaves and lectern.

Buddhistic Cross: see Swastika.

Buffet Car: a conventional symbol used particularly in continental railway timetables and indicating the provision of light refreshments service; see also Dining Car.

Built-up Fraction: that in which the figures denoting the numerator and denominator, and the horizontal dividing line, are separate pieces, and thus not quite the same as a split fraction.

1 _ 4 $\frac{1}{4}$

Bulgarian: a European language using the Cyrillic form of characters.

АБВГДЕЖЗИЙКЛМНОПРСТУФ
ХЦЧШЩЪЬѢЮЯѪ абвгдежзийк
лмнопрстуфхцчшщъьѣюяѫ

Butted: plain rule, made up as a box or border, having the constituent pieces coming flush against each other.

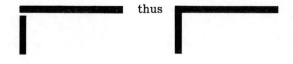

 thus 

C

C: the third letter of the English alphabet.

Cc Cc Cc Cc

Cadmium: a tin-like metal, of the magnesian group. (Cd)

Caduceus: the heraldic rod of Mercury, the messenger of the gods.

Caesium: a rare, alkali metal. (Cs)

Calcium: an alkaline earth metal. (Ca)

Calendar Figures: those cast as blocks on uniform widths and depths of body, and often surrounded with rule or background.

1						
	2	3	4	5	6	7
8	9	10	11	12	13	14
15	16	17	18	19	20	21
22	23	24	25	26	27	28
29	30					

Calendar Figures: CONTINUED

13 14 15 16 17 18 19

20 21 22 23 24 25 26

1 2 3 4 5 6 7

8 9 10 11

12 13

23/30 24/31 23/30 24/31

23/30 24/31 23/30 24/31

13 14 15 22 29

20 21 22

7 21 15 29

8 14 18 26

1 8 17 24

2 15 13 20

Californium: a radio-active element. (Cf)

Cameo: a type design appearing as white on a black background, also known as Reversed type.

GILL CAMEO

Cameo Lined: see Groundline.

Canal: a cartographical symbol.

Cancelled Figures: those through which a diagonal stroke is run; also known as Crossed, Erased or Scratched figures.

1234567890 1234567890

Cancer: see Zodiac, Signs of.

Caph: see Hebrew alphabet.

Capital Figures: see Lining figures.

Capitals: the largest letters, or majuscules, of the fount; of uniform height.

ABCDEFGHIJKLMNO
PQRSTUVWXYZ

ABCDEFGHIJKLMNOPQ
RSTUVWXYZ

Capitals: CONTINUED

ABCDEFGHIJKLMNOPQRST
UVWXYZ

ABCDEFGHIJKLMNOP
QRSTUVWXYZ

ABCDEFGHIJKLMNOPQR
STUVWXYZ

ABCDEFGHIJKLMNOPQRST
UVWXYZ

ABCDEFGHIJKL
MNOPQRSTUVW
XYZ

ABCDEFGHIJKLMNO
PQRSTUVWXYZ

ABCDEFGHIJKLMN
OPQRSTUVWXYZ

ABCDEFGHIJKLMNOP
QRSTUVWXYZ

Capitals: CONTINUED

ABCDEFGHIJKLMNOPQRST
UVWXYZ

ABCDEFGHIJKLMNOPQRSTUV
WXYZ

ABCDEFGHIJKLMNOP
QRSTUVWXYZ

ABCDEFGHIJKLMNOPQ
RSTUVWXYZ

ABCDEFGHIJKLMNOPQRS
TUVWXYZ

ABCDEFGHIJKLMNOPQRSTUVWXYZ

ABCDEFGHIJKLMNO
PQRSTUVWXYZ

ABCDEFGHIJKLMNOPQRS
TUVWXYZ

ABCDEFGHIJKLMNOPQRSTUV
WXYZ

Capitals: CONTINUED

ABCDEFGHIJKLMN
OPQRSTUVWXYZ

ABCDEFGHIJKLMNOP
QRSTUVWXYZ

ABCDEFGHIJKLMNOPQRST
UVWXYZ

ABCDEFGHIJKLMNOPQR
STUVWXYZ

Cap Line: the imaginary line at the top of the letters reached by the capitals.

Cap Line .... CAP LINE

Capricornus: see Zodiac, Signs of.

Capuchin Cross: a cross having each arm terminated by a ball.

Carbon: a chemical element. Ⓒ

Cardinal's Cross: see Patriarchal cross.

Card Pips: conventional symbols for hearts, diamonds, clubs and spades used on playing cards.

♥ ♦ ♣ ♠ ♡ ♢ ♧ ♤

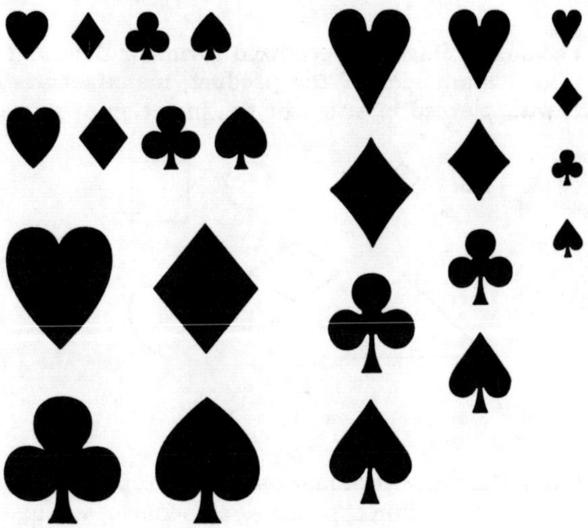

Care of: a commercial symbol-contraction.

℅ ℅ ℅ ℅ ℅ ℅

Caret: a symbol denoting something omitted. ∧

Cartographical Signs: conventional symbols used on maps; see under the names of the individual signs.

Castle[1]**:** a cartographical symbol. ■

Castle[2]**:** see Chess.

Catalogue: a medium weight of type, used primarily in catalogues and similar work.

Goudy Catalogue

Catalogue Marks: specialized forms or devices to convey an instant idea of the product, manufacturer's device, with pierced interior for the insertion of names, etc.

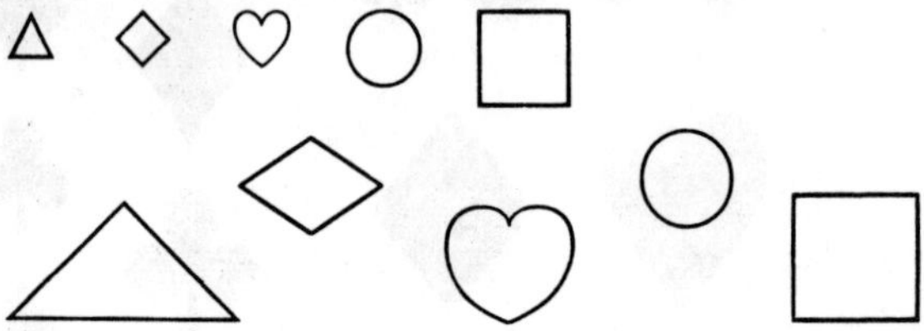

Cat's Ear: the termination at the top of the Capital C and G in certain type faces; also known as Lug.

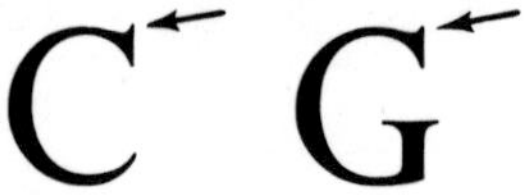

Caulocarp: a plant that bears fruit many times. 

Caution: a road sign warning of possible danger.

Cedilla: the accent used (particularly in French) below the letter C, to soften this letter.

ç Ç

Celtic Cross: a religious symbol in which the cross is surmounted by a ring; also known as Runic cross.

Celtic Ornament: that evolved by the Celts.

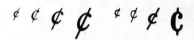

Cent: a symbol used in American and other currencies.

¢ ¢ ¢ ¢ ¢ ¢ ¢ ¢

Centimetre: a measurement in the metric system.

c/m c/m or cm

Ceres: see Asteroid.

Cerium: a rare-earth element. (Ce)

Chain: linking lines, as used in chemical formulae.

/ // \ \\

Character: see Sort.

Chemical Formulæ: see under individual names, e.g. Bond.

Chemist[1]: a scientist specializing in some branch of chemistry.

Chemist[2]: see Pharmacist.

Cheque Rule: a series of rules used on cheques, etc., often incorporating the pound sterling sign (see also Scroll).

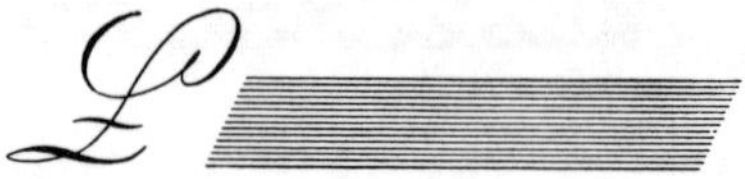

Cheques: see Scroll.

Chess: the conventionalized forms of chessmen with black and white squares, cast on em quad bodies and supplied in sets for building up into any desired plan of action.

Rook (or Castle)

Knight

Bishop

Queen

King

Pawn

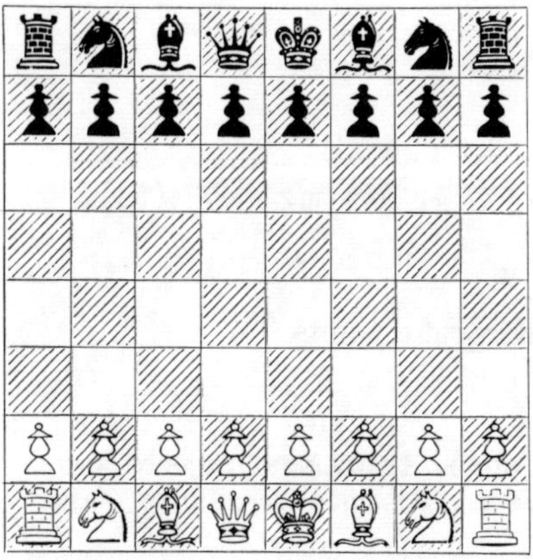

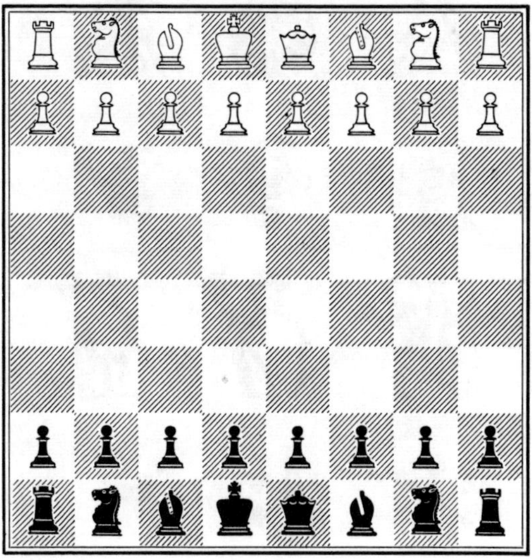

Cheth: see Hebrew alphabet.

Chevron: a V-shaped pattern used in heraldry, architecture, etc., of equal thickness throughout its form.

 or 

Chi: see Greek alphabet.

Chirek: see Masoretic points.

Chlorine: a heavy, suffocating gas. (Cl)

Cholem: see Masoretic points.

Christmas Symbols: traditional objects associated with the festival, e.g. Christmas tree, Santa Klaus.

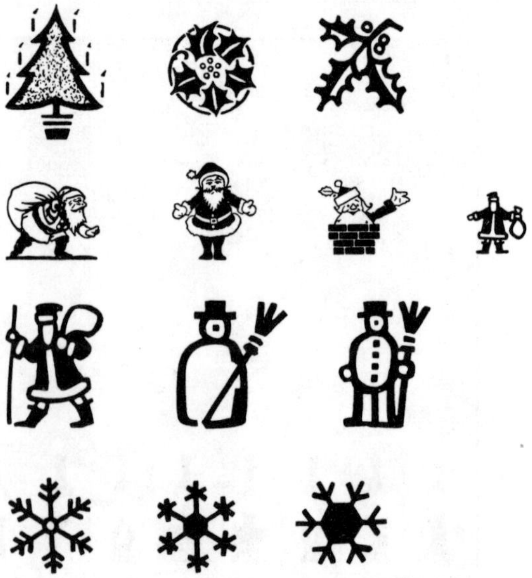

Christmas Symbols: CONTINUED

Christmas Tree: a yuletide ornament, often for two-colour printing.

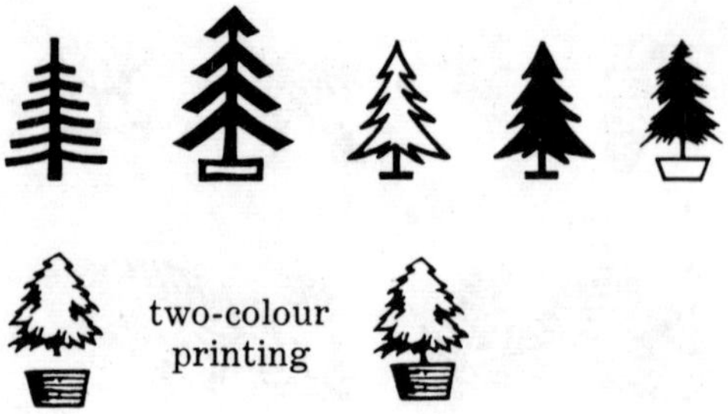

Chromium: a metallic element. Ⓒr

Church: a cartographical symbol. 

Church Text: see Black letter.

Cinema Signs: those used to indicate whether a film is for

Universal showing Ⓤ

Adults only Ⓐ

X certificate (Horror) Ⓧ

Circles: lead or brass hollow rings, etc., for the insertion of type matter; may be obtained completely circular or as semi-circular sections, mortised with square corners; procurable in various patterns.

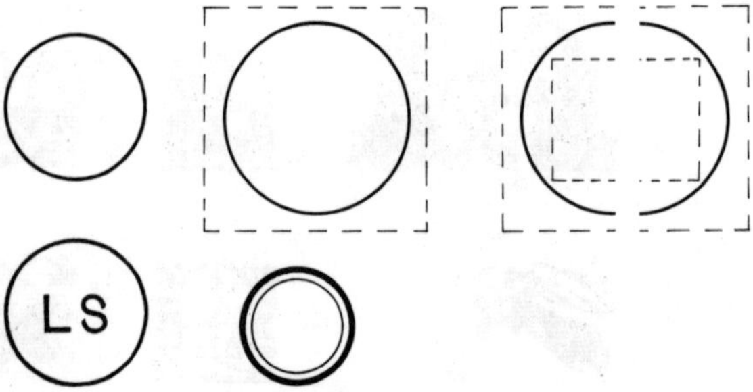

Circumflex: an accent used over the vowels and on some of the consonants; also called umbrella accent.

â ê î ô û ĉ ĝ ĥ ĵ ŝ ŵ ŷ ẑ

Clarendon: a medium weight, modified slab-serif type face, closely akin to Antique and Egyptian.

Craw Clarendon

Craw Clarendon Book

New Clarendon 617

CONSORT

CONSORT LIGHT

CONSORT BOLD

CONSORT BOLD CONDENSED

Volta

Clef: a symbol used in music to give name and pitch.

G clef

treble

F clef

bass

C clef

tenor

Climbing: indicated in botanical works by symbols

climbing ⌒ right hand **(** left hand **)**

Clockwise: a mathematical symbol. ↻

Closed h: a lower-case italic letter, with inward-turning stroke.

h

Cloud: see Sky.

Club: see Card pips.

Coat of Arms: a heraldic device for countries, county councils, corporations, etc.

Cobalt: a metallic element. (Co)

Cock-up Figures: see Superior figures.

Colon: a punctuation mark.

Mean Line.......●.................................

Base Line.......●.................................

Colones: a monetary symbol. ₡ ₡ ₡ ₡

Colophon: an ornamental tailpiece or device.

Combination Fractions: sets of figures (diagonal fractions, superior and inferior figures) used for making up odd fractional amounts.

$^1/_4$ $^1/_2$ $^3/_4$ $^1/_3$ $^2/_3$ $^1/_8$ $^3/_8$ $^5/_8$ $^7/_8$

$^1/_1$ $^3/_1$ $^5/_1$ $^7/_1$ $^9/_1$ $^3/_3$ $^5/_3$ $^7/_3$ $^9/_3$

$^1/_6$ $^3/_6$ $^5/_6$ $^7/_6$ $^9/_6$

^{1234567890} $_{1234567890}$

1 $^1/_4$ 2

$^{11}/_{42}$

Combination Type: see Interchangeable.

Comet: an astronomical symbol.  or 

Comma: a punctuation mark.

Base Line........,..................................

Commerce: a symbol used to indicate commerce in directories, in which composition space and time must be saved.

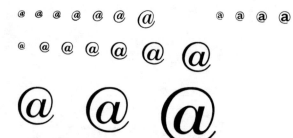

Commercial A: means at or to; also known as curly, round or short a.

@ @ @ @ @ @ @   @ @ @ @

@ @ @ @ @ @ @

@ @ @

Commercial Signs: see under individual names, e.g. Per cent, Commercial a, etc.

Commercial Stroke: see Separatrix.

Common Fractions: see Vulgar fractions.

Composer: a symbol used to indicate music composer in directories, in which composition space and time must be saved.

Compound Fractions: those bearing two figures in numerator or denominator; cast generally on em-quad body.

$\frac{1}{16}$ $\frac{15}{16}$

Compressed: a type considerably narrower than the standard.

CHELTENHAM BOLD COMPRESSED

Roman Compressed No. 3

Concave Serif: that with rounded ends and a centre depression or cup at the main stroke; see also Slur serif.

M

Condensed: where the set of a type is appreciably less than the normal, but not so narrow as compressed.

Condensa

Craw Clarendon Condensed

Latin Bold Condensed

Melior Bold Condensed

Plantin Bold Condensed

Standard Bold Condensed

Congruence: a mathematical symbol expressing agreement between certain figures or identical quality.

$\equiv$

Conjunction: the relation of certain planets at a given time.

☌

Consonant: a letter representing a speech sound uttered when the vocal current is impeded; in English, the following letters are so regarded:

bcdfghjklmnpqrstvwxyz

Contains: a mathematical symbol. $\succ$

Continuous Borders: those obtainable as lengths of printing equipment and showing a repeat pattern, continuous lines, etc.; also known as Strip Borders.

Contour Integral: a mathematical symbol. $\oint$

Convex Serif: see Slur serif.

Copper: a ductile metal; takes its symbol from the Latin word Cuprum.

(Cu)

Copperplate: see Script.

Corner Piece: a decorative or other printing element used to embellish or complete the joins of borders.

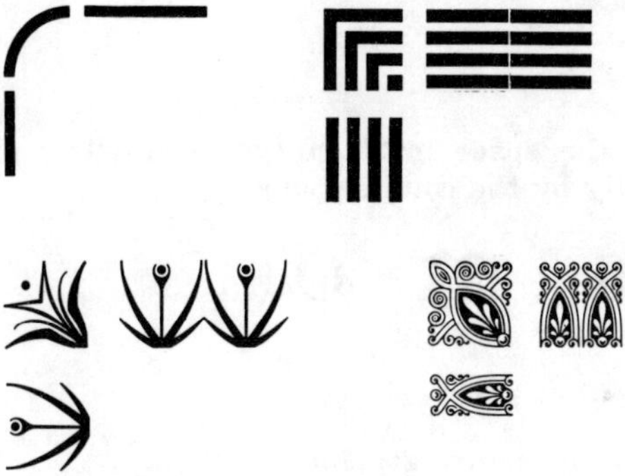

Corona[1]**:** an astronomical halo.

lunar corona   solar corona ⦶

lunar halo    solar halo ⊕

Corona[2]**:** see Pause.

Coronet: a small crown, and an emblem of nobility.

Coronis: a Greek mark of contraction or uniting of two words into one.

π᾽ TOÛT' (=TOÛTO)

Cotyledon: the seed-leaf of an embryo plant.

accumbent lies along edges O=

incumbent lies against inner side O||

Couchette: a conventional symbol, used particularly in continental railway timetables, indicating a wagon with convertible accommodation for comfortable night travel; see also Sleeping car.

Counter: the space inside a type character, produced originally by the counter-punch.

County Town: a cartographical symbol.

⦿ or CT

Creditor: a contraction used in commercial work, statements, etc.

Crescendo: an instruction in music to denote increase.

Croatian Accents: čćđšž ČĆĐŠŽ

Crooked Cross: see Swastika.

Crossbar: see Bar[1].

Cross Crosslet: a cross decorated at its extremities.

Crossed Swords: see Battle.

Crossed Type: see Erased type; Scratched figures.

Crosses: ecclesiastical, etc., symbols of various design; see under particular names.

Cross Stem: one, particularly in W, where the centre arms pass over each other.

W

Crossword Puzzle: sets of black and white squares, figures, etc., for making up crossword puzzles to any desired pattern.

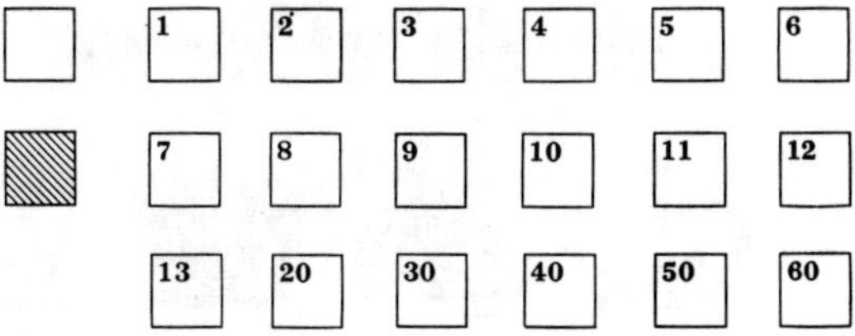

Crossword Puzzle: CONTINUED

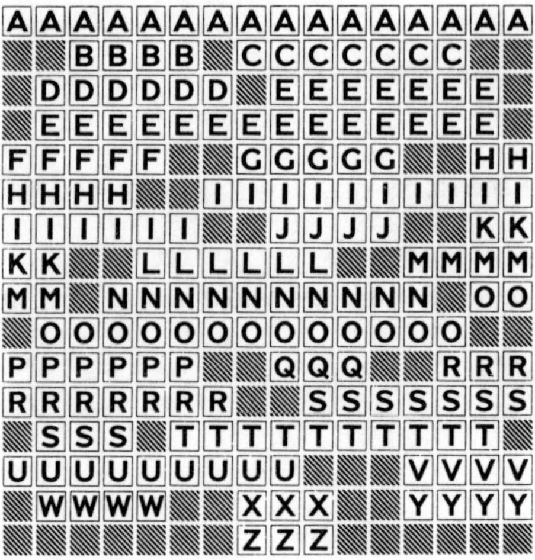

Crotch: the point of angle made by two strokes in the counter of a letter.

Crotchet[1]**:** a black, tailed note in music, one-half the value of a minim.

Crotchet[2] **(or Crotch):** see Bracket[1].

Crown: the emblem of sovereignty.

Crowned M: a religious sign. 

Crux Ansata: a cross with a handle. 

Crux Commissa: see St. Anthony's Cross.

Crux Decussata: a cross in the shape of a saltire; also known as Oblique cross; St. Andrew's cross, St. Patrick's cross.

X

Crux Immissa: see Latin cross.

Crux Stellata: a cross the arms of which terminate with stars.

Cube: a figure consisting of six surfaces of the same size, but rendered typographically as four squares within a large square.

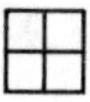 [also ]

Cube Border: one in which part of the cubic figure appears.

Cube Root: a number which multiplied by itself three times produces a given cube; e.g. $4 \times 4 \times 4 = 64$, thus 4 is the cube root of 64.

$$\sqrt[3]{}$$

Cuneiform: wedge-shaped characters, as used in Babylonian.

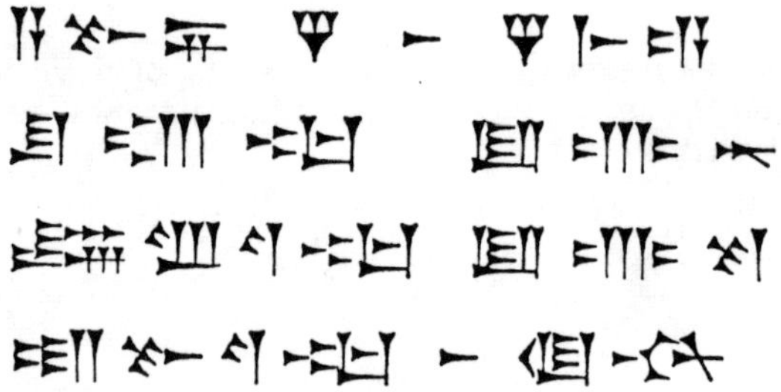

Cup: the depression at the head or foot of certain characters, particularly those with concave serifs.

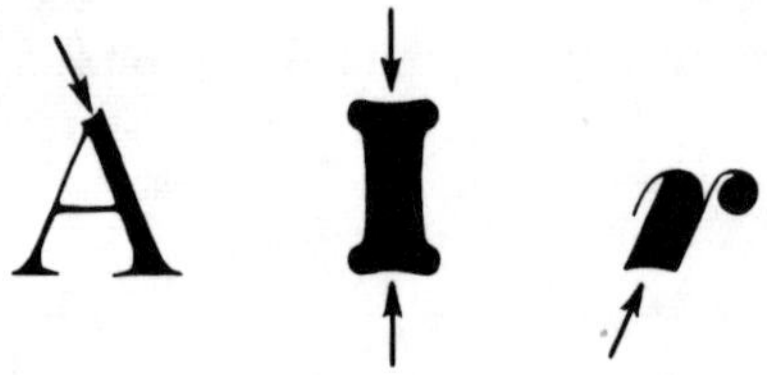

Cup and Ball Border: see Egg and dart border.

Curium: a transuranic radio-active element. (Cm)

Curly: applied to type designs which are very flowing.

Curly A: see Commercial a.

Curly And: see Ampersand.

Curly N: see Tilde.

Curly O: see Tilde.

Curly Q: the capital letter Q with elaborate tail.

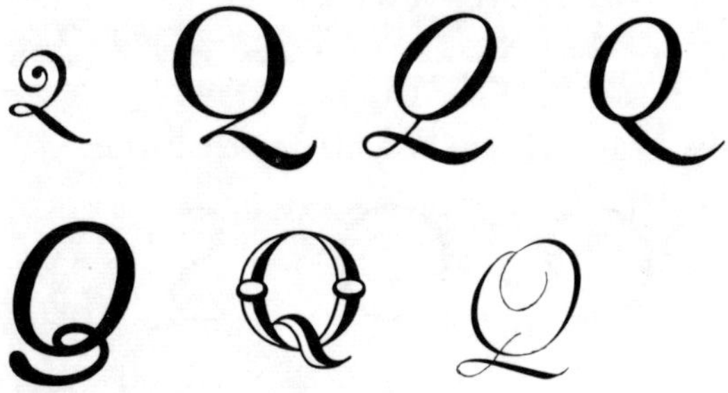

Curly Tail: an elaborate ending to a letter (see also Curly Q).

Currency Symbols: see under individual names, e.g. Pound, Dollar, Cent, etc.

Cursive: a flowing form of letter; often as imitation running handwriting or florid italic design.

Bernhard Cursive Bold

Goudy Cursive

Lydian Cursive

Raleigh Cursive

Sterling Cursive

Curve: a bowed line in a printed character.

C O S

Curves: arcs of various kinds, for use in geometry, mathematics, etc.

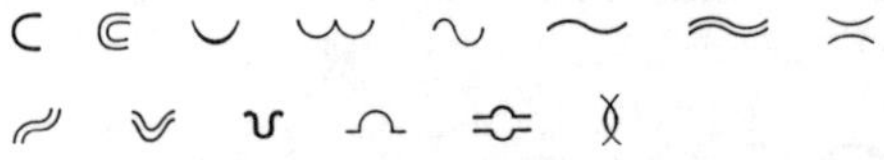

Customs: a symbol indicating frontier, especially in regard to railway and other timetables in Europe (also known as Douane).

Cypher: see Nullo.

Cyrillic: see Russian.

Czech Accents: those of the Bohemian peoples.

á č ď é ě í ň ó ř š ť ú ů ý ž

Á Č Ď É Ě Í Ň Ó Ř Š Ť Ú Ů Ý Ž

Czech U: see Czech Accents.

D

D: the fourth letter of the English alphabet.

Dd Dd *Dd* Dd

Dagesh: see Hebrew alphabet.

Dagger: the second bookwork reference mark; also used to indicate decease; known also as obelisk or obelus.

Daleth: see Hebrew alphabet.

Danish O: the letter O struck through with a diagonal line; also used in Norwegian.

Ø

Dash[1]**:** a symbol used in music to indicate very staccato playing.

'

Dash[2]**:** see Em rule; Metal rule; Ornamental dash; Pen dash; Swelled Rule.

Death: see Decease.

Debtor: a contraction used in commercial work, statements, etc.

Decease: the sign placed alongside a name to indicate deceased person.

†

Decimal Fractions: those expressed under the decimal system; the figures to the right of the decimal point, a nullo should be inserted wherever appropriate to the left of the point.

0·27

Decimal Point: see En dot.

Decorated Letters: see Fancy type faces.

Decrease: see Decrescendo.

Decrescendo: an instruction in music to denote decrease.

Degree: a symbol of gradation used in mathematics, etc.

° (100°)

Dele (or Delete): the symbol used by printers to denote take out or remove.

δ

Delta: see Greek alphabet.

Demisemiquaver: a black, stemmed note in music, with three lines on stem, one-half the value of the semiquaver.

Descender: a lower-case letter with a descending stroke or tail, or the tail itself.

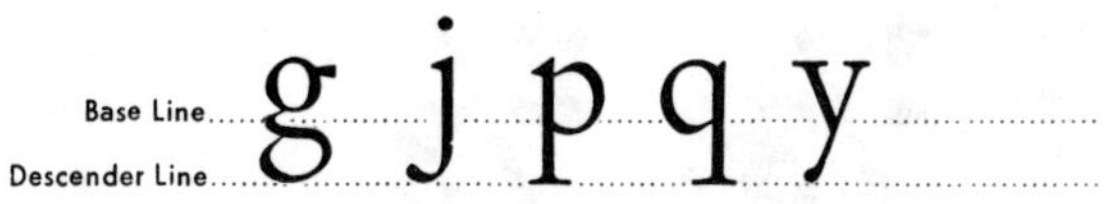

Descender Line: the imaginary line to which descending strokes reach.

Dew: a meteorological symbol. ⌓

Diacritics: symbols used to distinguish between values of a given letter,

e.g. è é ë etc.

Diaeresis Accent: used to denote separate enunciation of two adjacent vowels or to modify the sound.

ä ë ï ö ü

Diagonal: see Separatrix.

Diagonal Fractions: those having a diagonal line between the numerator and the denominator; generally, though not always, cast on em quad body; also called old style or sloping fractions.

1/2 1/3 2/3 1/4 3/4 1/8 3/8 5/8 7/8

1/16 3/16 5/16 7/16 9/16 1/32 1/64

1/4 1/2 3/4

1/3 2/3

1/5 4/5

Diamond: see Card pips.

Diamond Rule: one consisting of a fine, horizontal line, in the centre of which appears a diamond; used extensively in newspaper make-up; also known as French rule.

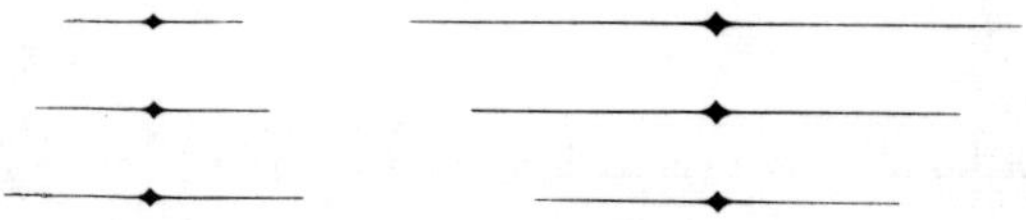

Diamonds: open, solid or figured signs of conventional shape, as used in geometry, etc.

Dice: representations of dice, as used in games of chance.

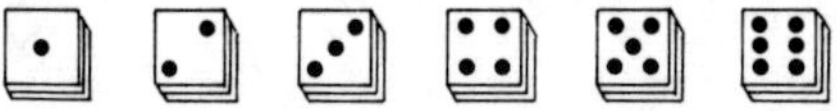

Diesis: see Double dagger.

Difference Between: a mathematical symbol. $\sim$

Differential: a mathematical symbol. $\partial\ \Delta$ or d

Digamma Function: a mathematical symbol. F

Digits[1]**:** the symbol for the word ditto, and consisting normally of two commas close together.

”

Digits[2]: the name for any figures.   **1 2 3** etc.

Dining Car: a conventional symbol used particularly in Continental railway timetables and indicating a full meals service; see also Buffet car.

Diphthong: the printer's name for the vowel ligatures.

æœ ÆŒ   æœ ÆŒ   *æœ ÆŒ*   æœ ÆŒ   **æœÆŒ**

Direction: signs used to point the way, and consisting of arrowheads and lines variously arranged.

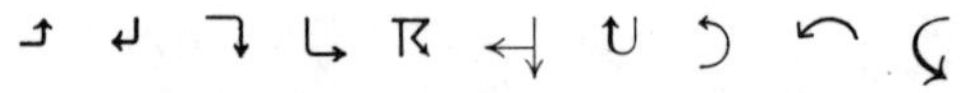

Display Brackets: those designed, usually in large sizes, for ornamental purposes, to surround panels of type matter, etc.

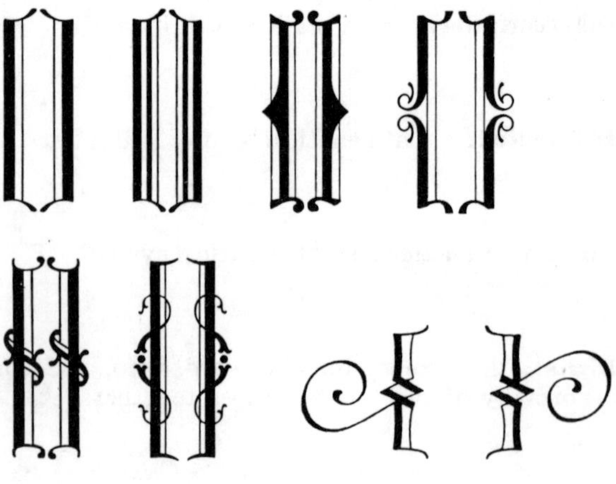

Display Types: those used for emphasizing the message; their range is very extensive and they usually possess decorative qualities that make them suitable for advertisement and publicity work; also called Jobbing types.

Ad Lib

ALLRIGHT

Ashley Script

BETON OPEN

Braggadocio

Century Oldstyle Bold

Chisel

Clarendon Bold

COLONNA

COLUMNA

CRISTAL

Echo

ELONGATED ROMAN

FESTIVAL

GILL SANS ULTRA BOLD

HESS NEOBOLD

OLD BOWERY

ORPLID

OTHELLO

Pepita

PRISMA

REGINA

SOLEMNIS

STOP

STREAMLINE

Thorowgood Italic

Time Script

Whitin Black Condensed

Zebra

ZEPHYR

Ditto: see Digits[1]; Nuller.

Division: the mathematical symbol of dividing.

÷ ÷ ÷ ÷ ÷ ÷ ÷

÷ ÷ ÷ ÷ ÷ ÷

Dollar: a symbol used in American and other currencies.

$ $ $ $ $ $ $ $

Domesday Signs: see Scribal Abbreviations.

Dominoes: a representation of the pieces in a set of dominoes.

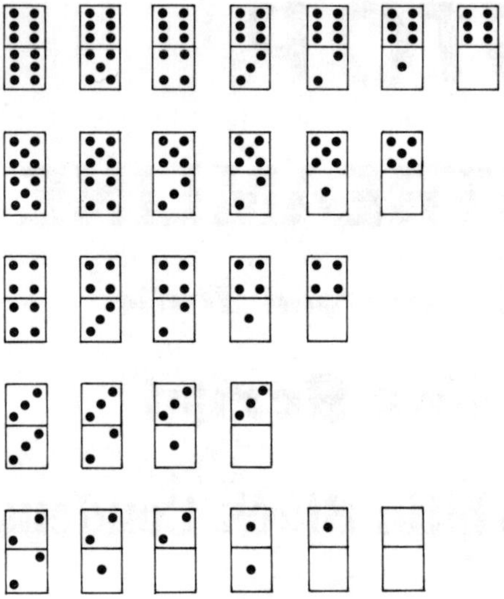

Doomsday Signs: see Scribal Abbreviations.

Doric: a square-faced, sanserif type; made in various weights.

DORIC

DORIC No. 1 ITALIC

Dot[1]**:** the small point above the lower-case i and j.

Dot[2]**:** an advertising device in the form of a solid circle; also known as Black dot.

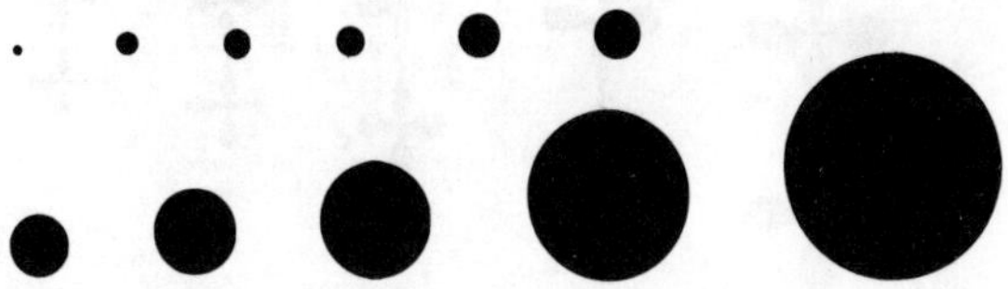

Dot[3]**:** see Ball.

Dotted Figures: those used (inter alia) to denote recurring decimals.

1̇2̇3̇4̇5̇6̇7̇8̇9̇0̇ **1̇2̇3̇4̇5̇6̇7̇8̇9̇0̇**

Dotted Letters: those with a small point above them.

ȧḃċḋėḟġḣijk̇l̇ṁṅȯṗq̇ṙṡṫu̇v̇ẇẋẏż

ȦḂĊḊĖḞĠḢİJ̇K̇L̇ṀṄȮṖQ̇ṘṠṪU̇V̇ẆẊẎŻ

Douane: see Customs.

Double Bars: a double perpendicular line used to mark a division of the musical stave.

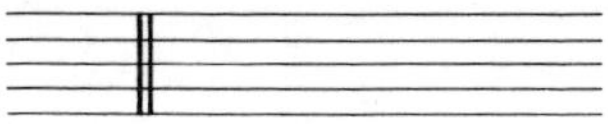

Double Contour Integral: a mathematical symbol. $\oiint$

Double Cross: see Patriarchal cross.

Double Dagger: the third bookwork reference mark; also known as the diesis or double obelisk.

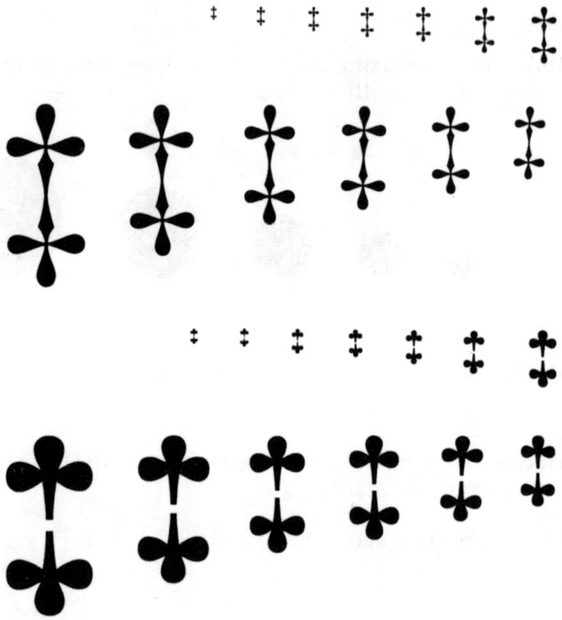

Double Flat: a symbol used in music. 𝄫

Double Jerusalem Cross: an ecclesiastical symbol, upon the main arms of which are arranged smaller crosses.

Double Letters: see Diphthongs; Ligatures.

Double Obelisk: see Double dagger.

Double Quotation Marks: see Quotation marks.

Double Reversed Arrow: a pair of arrows laid together horizontally with their barbs at opposite ends. (See Reversible reaction.)

⇆

Double Rule: that composed of two lines of the same or different weight or design.

Double S: a pair of s characters joined (as in German).

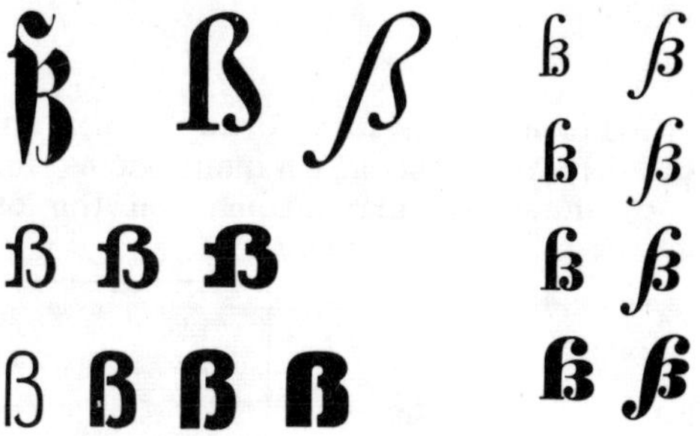

Double Sharp: a symbol placed before a note already sharp to raise its pitch a semi-tone.

×

Doubtful Length: a combination of the short and the long accent.

ā̆

Downstroke: that formed by a downward stroke of the pen, and thus normally the heavy stroke.

Drachm: a medical symbol. ʒ

Dragon's Head: see Node (ascending).

Dragon's Tail: see Node (descending).

Drama: see Actor.

Draughts: symbols representing draughtsmen and black and white squares, cast on em-quad bodies, for building up to show any arrangement on the draughts board.

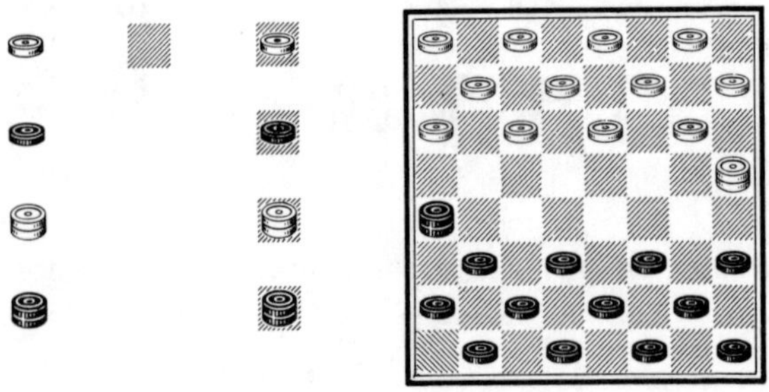

Draughts: CONTINUED

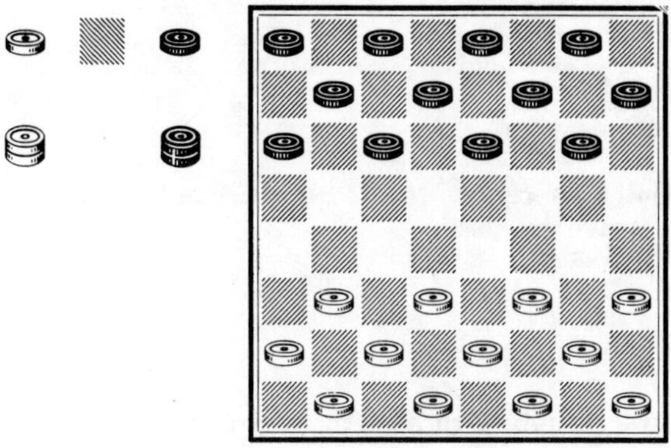

Drizzle: a meteorological symbol. ,

Drop Figures: those of old style design that descend below the base line.

Mean Line....I..............34579..............
Base Line....

Drop Initials: letters of large size inserted at the beginning of a section of text matter and covering the depth of a number of lines.

THE letters inserted at the beginning
of a section of text matter
and covering the depth
of a number of lines.

Druggist: see Apothecary.

Drug Marks: pharmacists' stock symbols or words.

P1 S1 DD P1 P2 S1 DD S1P2

P1 P1 S1 S4 P1 P2 DD D.D.A S.S.

POISON POISON POISONOUS

Dust: meteorological symbols, varying according to intensity.

§ devil   S→ storm

Dutch Accents: the acute, circumflex, diaeresis, and grave are used.

èéêëòóô ÈÉÊËÒÓÔ

Dysprosium: a rare-earth element. Ⓓy

E

E: the fifth letter of the English alphabet.

Ee Ee Ee Ee

Ear: the slur or ball terminals of lower-case g, r, etc.

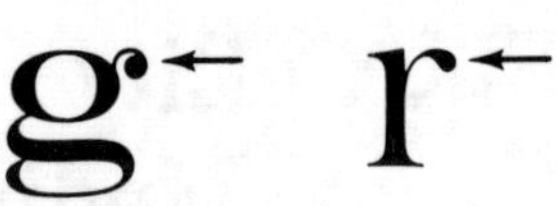

Earth: an astronomical symbol. ⊖ or ⊕

Earth and Moon: a combined astronomical symbol. ♁

Eccentricity, Angle of: an astronomical symbol. ∅

Ecclesiastical Symbols: see under individual names, e.g. Crowned M, Greek Cross, etc.

Egg and Dart Border: an ornament comprising these two designs; also known as Cup and ball border.

Egyptian: a type face of rather stiff design, with square serifs; akin to Antique and Clarendon.

Egyptian Expanded

KARNAK INTERMEDIATE

Scarab Bold

ROCKWELL

City Medium

TOWER

Stymie Bold

CAIRO BOLD

Playbill

FIGARO

CLARENCE CONDENSED

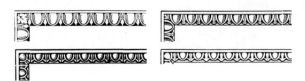

Egyptian Cross: see St. Anthony's cross.

Eight: the symbol for an octuple quantity.

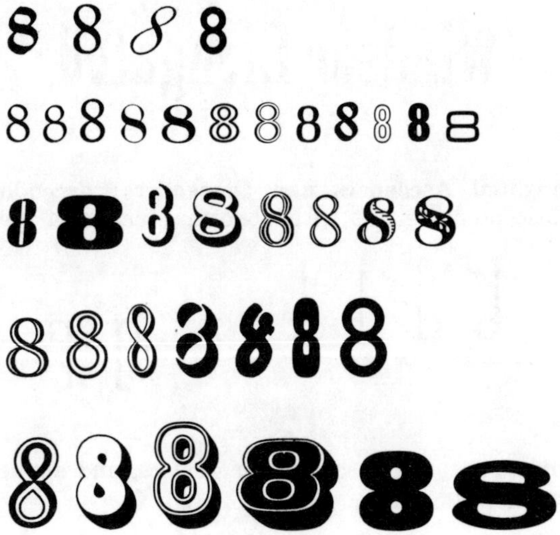

Eight-Pointed Cross: see Maltese cross.

Electoral Signs: see Ballot Paper Signs.

Electronic Figures: those of specialized form to permit of the operation of computing machines.

1 2 3 4 5 6 7 8 9 0

Elephant: an extreme degree of boldness in a type face.

GRANBY ELEPHANT

Ellipsis: see Points.

Elongated: a very compressed type.

ELONGATED ROMAN

Windsor Elongated

Elongated Ascenders and Descenders: ascending and descending letters with abnormal length of stroke.

b d h k x q p y

Emblems: symbolic badges or devices, and applicable to many subjects.

Em Rule: a horizontal line usually cast centrally on a one-em body. (See also Metal rule.)

Encircled Figures/Letters: see Ringed figures/letters.

En Dot: a dot cast in the centre of an en body, and serving as a decimal point.

Engine: see Train.

Engineer: a symbol used to indicate engineer in directories, in which composition space and time must be saved.

Engraved: a heavy face type, relieved with fine line.

BROADWAY
ENGRAVED

En Quad Fractions: see Straight fractions.

En Rule: a single, horizontal line cast centrally on the body an en quad wide.

Entomologist: a symbol used to indicate entomologist in directories, in which composition space and time must be saved.

Epsilon: see Greek alphabet.

Equal: the symbol of equality.

= = = = = = = =
= = = = = =

Equal and Parallel: a mathematical symbol. ⋕

Equiangular: a mathematical symbol. ≚

Equilateral: a mathematical symbol. ⊥

Equivalent to: a mathematical symbol. ≍

Erased Type: that through which a line is cast to give the appearance of cancelling.

~~abcdefghijklmnopqrstuvwxyz~~ ~~1234567890~~

~~ABCDEFGHIJKLMNOPQRSTUVWXYZ~~

Erbium: a rare-earth element. (Er)

Ermine: a heraldic symbol. 

Erse: see Gaelic.

Esperanto: an international language; accents used are circumflex and short.

ĉĝĥĵŝŭ ĈĜĤĴŜŬ

Eta: see Greek alphabet.

Etcetera: see Andcetera.

Eth: an Anglo-Saxon character designating th as in the; not to be confused with Thorn (q.v.); used also in Icelandic.

ð Ð

Europium: a rare-earth element. (Eu)

Evergreen: a plant that is green all the year round. △

Exclamation: a punctuation mark to denote emotion; also called note of admiration, screamer or squealer.

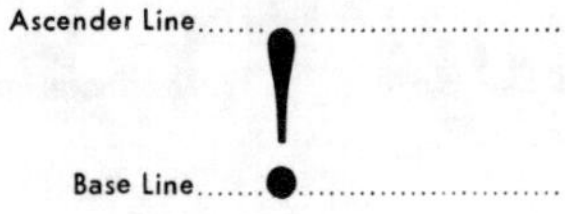

Exotic: descriptive of florid, unusual renderings of the Latin alphabet, or non-European forms.

assignment

Art News

profession

against any

accepts

Lettering

illustrations

Exotic: CONTINUED

Arabic

بنط ٣٦ مونوتيب عر

Chinese

靈我可眞

Greek

αὐτόν. ἐμοὶ δὲ ἀρκοῦν ἂν ἐδόκει εἶναι ἀνδρ
ΟΙ ΜΕΝ ΠΟΛΛΟΙ ΤΩΝ ΕΝΘΑΔΕ ΗΔΗ

Hebrew (Pointed)

פִּים לַמַּחֲרֵשׁוֹת וְלָאֵתִים

Sanskrit (Devanagari)

वन्नियम : । उत स्वित्परिसंख्या ? । तत्र विधिरप्राप्ते थवति
यावजीवमग्निहोत्रं जुहोति इत्यादि सर्वम । यस्मिन्प्राप्ते

Tamil

த்திற்கொப்பாகிய அன்னக் குவியலையும் பசஷிண
சனங்களையும் லேகிய சோஷியங்களையும் வெய்ய

Turkish

جغئآش

Urdu

لاهور میں راج کرتا تھا - جب اُس نے اسلام
زور هندوستان کی طرف بڑھتا دیکھا - تو اُس

Expanded: type considerably wider than the standard.

EGYPTIAN
EXPANDED

Chatsworth Expanded

CHELTENHAM BOLD
EXPANDED

SPARTAN BOLD EXPANDED

Expanding Brace/Bracket: see Brace/Bracket.

Exponent: see Superior figures/letters.

Extended: a type much wider than the standard.

Albion Extended

Record Gothic Extended

Standard Extended

Extra Bold: a weight of type between bold and ultra.

CLEARFACE EXTRA BOLD

Folio Extrabold

Fortune Extrabold

SPARTAN EXTRA BOLD

Venus Extrabold

VERONA EXTRA BOLD

Extra Condensed: a type considerably narrower than normal.

GILL SANS BOLD EXTRA CONDENSED

Placard Light EXTRA Condensed

Record Gothic Extra Condensed

Extra Light: a weight of type much thinner than the normal.

Standard Extralight Extended

Extruder: that part of a letter extending from the main portion, as in

Eye: the enclosed counter in a lower-case e. 

Eyecatcher: a distinctive or prominent feature of a type, often serving as a means of identification.

F

F: the sixth letter of the English alphabet.

Ff Ff Ff Ff

Face[1]: the printing portion of the letter.

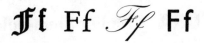

Face[2]: the characteristics inherent in the design of a type, and distinguishing it from others.

ALBERTUS

Ancient Black BOLOGNA

COLONNA

ELONGATED ROMAN

Fry's Baskerville

GALLIA Gavotte

Gill Sans Shadow Line

GRANBY Hyperion

Information

Kennerley Klang

MATURA Melior Semi-bold

MICHELANGELO

NEULAND

OFFENBACH

Ornata

Playbill RICCARDO

Temple Script Virtuosa I

Windsor

Factorial: an expression of mathematical notation,

e.g. $\lfloor\underline{n}$ or $n!$

Factotum Initial: a large initial cut away for the insertion of any desired wording.

Fadeaway Dash: see Swelled rule.

Family: the various type faces of a particular design, modified for particular purposes.

Folio Light

Folio Light Italic

Folio Light Condensed

Folio Medium

Folio Medium Condensed

Folio Medium Extended

Folio Medium Extended Italic

Folio Bold

Folio Bold Condensed

Folio Bold Condensed Italic

Family: CONTINUED

Folio Bold Extra Condensed

Folio Bold Extended

Folio Extrabold

Fancy Type Faces: those possessing unusual adornment or decoration.

ARBORET

CICERO CORINTHIAN

DIAMOND JIM

DRESDEN

FARGO FLORADORA

FONTANESI

FOURNIER

GRECO ADORNADO

LEXINGTON

Fancy Type Faces: CONTINUED

Lilith MANDARIN

MODERNISTIC

ODYSSEY

OMBRE

Ornata

ROMANTIQUE NO. 1

RUSTIC

SAPPHIRE

SOUTHERN CROSS

THUNDERBIRD

TROCADERO

Union Pearl

Farad: an electrical symbol of capacity. ϕ

Fat[1]**:** a type with a wide set.

Paragon

abcdefghijklmnopqrstuvwxyz

ABCDEFGHIJKLMNOPQRSTUVWXYZ

Fat[2]**:** a type with rather heavy stems and light serifs or bars.

Falstaff

Normande

Thorowgood

Ultra Bodoni

Female: a natural history symbol. ♀

Figures: see Calendar figures; Inferior; Lining figures; Old Style figures; Overlined figures; Reversed figures; Ringed; Roman numerals; Scratched; Superior; Underlined.

Filet: see Bracket[2].

Filigree Initials: those surrounded with fine lines.

Filigree Initials: CONTINUED

Fillet: see Bracket[2].

Final Letters: see Hebrew alphabet; Word terminals.

Fine Face Rule: that showing a face of hair line thickness.

Fine Serif: one consisting of a very light line.

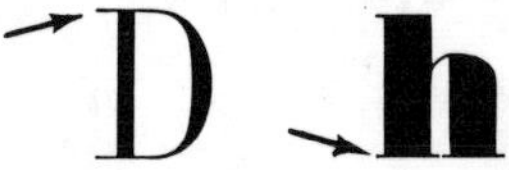

Finial[1]**:** an end-piece, especially in the form of a bunch of foliage.

Finial[2]: see Word terminals.

Finite Difference: an algebraical symbol. △

Finnish Accents: diaeresis and Swedish A. äåö ÄÅÖ

Fish: conventional signs, often used in guide books, to indicate fishing rights, etc.

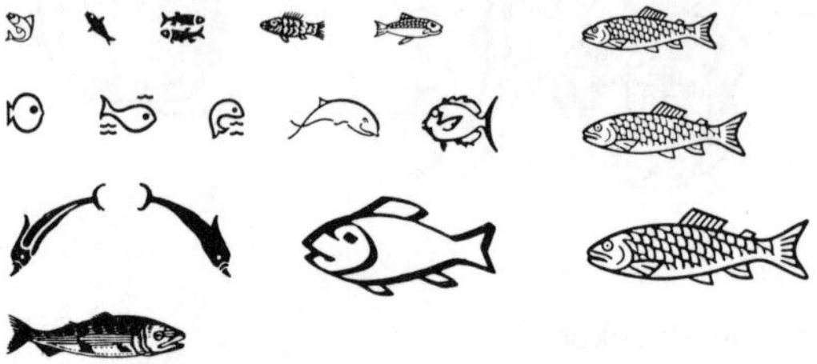

Fist: see Index[1].

Five: the symbol for a quintuple quantity.

5 5 5 5

5 5 5 5 5 5 5 5 5 5 5 5

5 5 5 5 5 5 5 5

5 5 5 5 5 5 5

5 5 5 5 5 5

Fixed Star: one that seems always to be in the same position.

☀ or ✳

Flag: a stylized form of national standard, often as separate pieces to allow of printing in the appropriate colours.

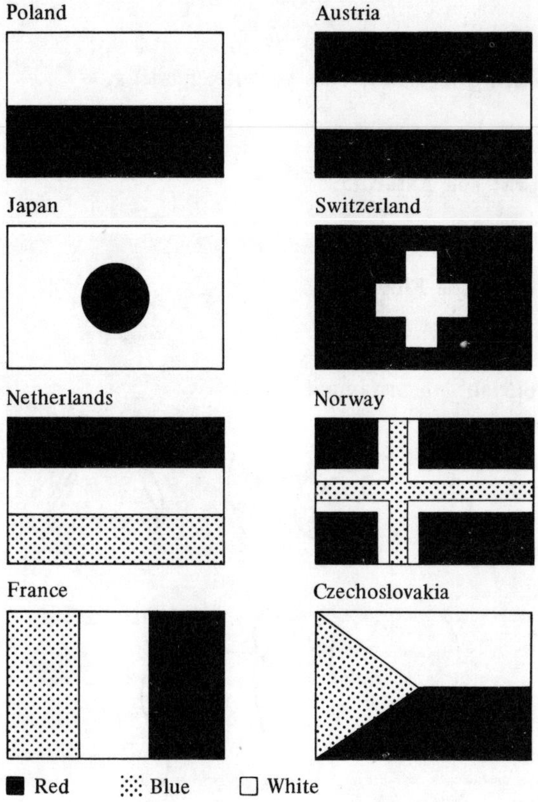

Poland

Austria

Japan

Switzerland

Netherlands

Norway

France

Czechoslovakia

■ Red ░ Blue □ White

Flat[1]: a symbol used in music to lower a note by a semitone.

♭

Flat[2]: see Slab Serif.

Fleur-de-lis: the symbol used in heraldry for the lily.

Floating Accents: see Accents, floating.

Flora: see Asteroid.

Floret: see Flowers.

Flourish: an ornamental line.

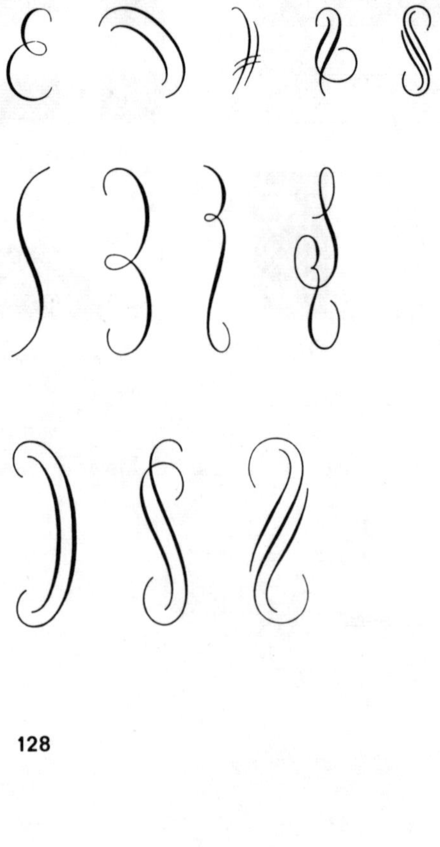

Flowers: ornaments of various patterns, free and florid in design.

Fluent: see Integration.

Fluorine: a gaseous element. Ⓕ

Fog: a meteorological symbol. ≡

=	≡
shallow	ground

Foot[1]: the base of a printing character.

Foot[2]**:** a mathematical symbol indicating measurement in foot (or feet).

′

Former: the ornamental or decorative surround to an initial letter; see Background.

Forte: a direction used in music (=strongly, loudly).

f

Fortissimo: a direction used in music (=very strongly, very loudly).

ff

Fortississimo: a direction in music (=as loud as possible).

fff

Fount: a collection of sorts, made up in the number of its individual characters according to frequency of use. A display fount usually contains the following:

aaaaa bbb cccdd
deeeeeeeffffgggh
hhiiiiijjkklllllmm
mnnnnoooopppq
rrrrsssstttttuuuvv
wwxxyyyz

Fount: CONTINUED

AAABBCCDDEE
EEFFGGHHIIIJJ
KKLLLMMNNN
OOOPPQRRRS
SSTTTUUVVW
WXYYZ&&£(())
,,,,,,......;;::''''----!!??
1112233445566
7788999000

Four: the symbol for a quadruple quantity.

4 4 4 4

4 4 4 4 4 4 4 4 4 4 4 4

4 4 4 4 4 4 4 4

4 4 4 4 4 4 4

4 4 4 4 4 4

Four-Pointed Star: a stylized form of display ornament.

Fractions: see Built-up fractions; Combination fractions; Compound fractions; Decimal fractions; Diagonal fractions; Improper fractions; Solid fractions; Split fractions; Straight fractions; Vulgar fractions.

Fraktur: a rather condensed angular form of German black letter.

Fette Altfraktur

abcdefghijklmn

opqrſstuvwxyz

ABCDEFG

HIKLMNO

PQRSTUV

WXYZ

Francium: a radio-active element. Ⓕr

French Accents: those used are the acute, cedilla, circumflex, diaeresis and grave.

àâçèéêëîïôùûü

ÀÂÇÈÉÊËÎÏÔÙÛÜ

French Rule: see Diamond rule.

Frontier: see Customs.

Frost: a meteorological symbol.

hoar	glazed	hard rime	soft rime
⊔	∾	▼	V

Frutex: the botanical symbol for a shrub. ♄

Full-Faced: see Titling.

Full Point: a punctuation point used at the end of sentences, in abbreviations, etc.; also called full stop or period.

Base Line......●..................

Fylfot: see Swastika.

G

G: the seventh letter of the English alphabet.

Gg Gg Gg Gg

Gadolinium: a rare-earth element. (Gd)

Gaelic: the language of the Gaels; Irish; the alphabet of which is beautifully symmetrical; also known as Erse or Irish.

abcdefghilmnopr
stu
áḃċḋéḟġíṁóṗṡṫú
abcdefghilmn
oprstu
áḃċḋéḟġíṁóṗṡ
ṫú

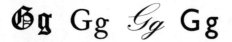

Gale: a meteorological symbol. 

Gallium: a metallic element. (Ga)

Gamma: see Greek alphabet.

Gammadion: see Swastika.

Gamma Function: a mathematical symbol. Γ

Gauge: the length of a character from top to bottom.

Gemini: see Zodiac, Signs of.

Geneva Cross: one similar in design to the Greek cross (q.v.).

Geographer: a symbol used to indicate geographer in directories, in which composition space and time must be saved. 

Geologist: a symbol used to indicate geologist in directories, in which composition space and time must be saved.

 or 

Geometrical Proportion: where the ratios in its two parts are equal, e.g., 2 : 4 :: 6 : 12 (as 2 is to 4 so is 6 to 12).

 or ∷

Geometrical Signs: see under individual names, e.g. Rectangle, Rhombus, etc.

German Accents: the diaeresis (German=Umlaut) is used.

ä ö ü   Ä Ö Ü

Germanium: a metallic element. (Ge)

Gimel: see Hebrew alphabet.

Glagolitic: derived from the Glagol alphabet, used among some Slavonic tribes.

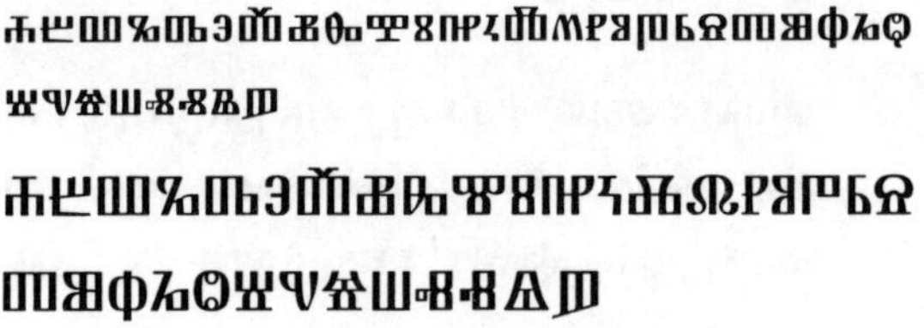

Glazed Frost: see Frost.

Gold: a precious metal; takes its symbol from the Latin word Aurum=gold.

(Au)

Gothic[1]**:** a sanserif letter of rather bold, square design; formerly, the name given to black letter types (q.v.).

Advertisers Gothic

AGENCY GOTHIC

Gothic[1]**:** CONTINUED

BANK GOTHIC MEDIUM

Gothic Bold 150

GOTHIC NO. 520

Lightline Gothic

Old Gothic Bold Italic

Record Gothic

Times Gothic

Gothic[2]**:** the language of the Goths, an early Teutonic tribe.

𐌸𐌹𐌿𐌳𐌹𐌽𐌰𐍃𐍃𐌿𐍃 𐌸𐌴𐌹𐌽𐍃: 𐍅𐌰𐌹𐍂𐌸𐌰𐌹 𐍅𐌹𐌻𐌾𐌰 𐌸𐌴𐌹𐌽𐍃
𐌰𐌽𐌰 𐌰𐌹𐍂𐌸𐌰𐌹: 𐌷𐌻𐌰𐌹𐍆 𐌿𐌽𐍃𐌰𐍂𐌰𐌽𐌰 𐌸𐌰𐌽𐌰 𐍃𐌹𐌽𐍄𐌴𐌹𐌽𐌰𐌽
𐌳𐌰𐌲𐌰: 𐌾𐌰𐌷 𐌰𐍆𐌻𐌴𐍄 𐌿𐌽𐍃 𐌸𐌰𐍄𐌴𐌹 𐍃𐌺𐌿𐌻𐌰𐌽𐍃

Grace Notes: small notes used in music to indicate embellishment.

Graphical Formula: a chemical formula made up of bonds, etc., as well as symbols.

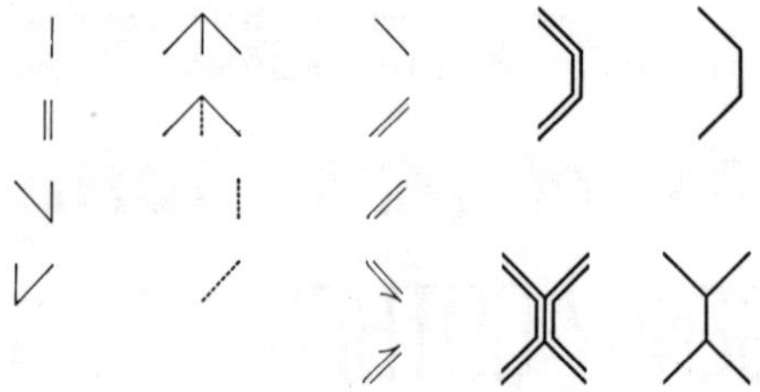

Graphical Formula: CONTINUED

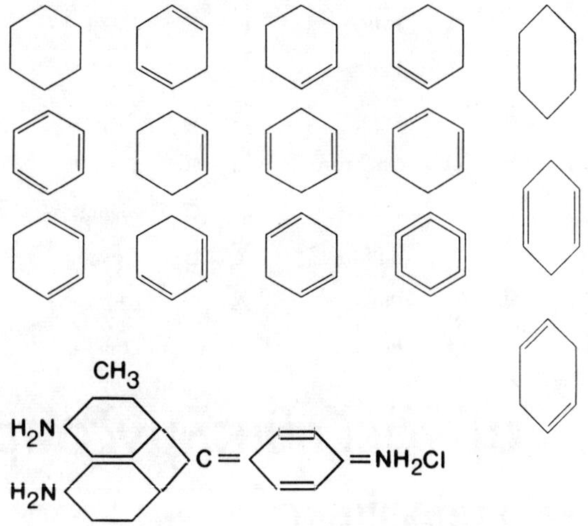

Grave Accent: that used on the vowels, sloping up from right to left.

à è ì ò ù

Greater or Less: a mathematical symbol. $\gtrless$

Greater Than: a mathematical symbol. $>$

Greater Than or Equal to: a mathematical symbol. $\geqq$

Greek Alphabet: consists of 24 letters; there are various punctuation and other points.

Α	α	Alpha	Β	β	Beta
Γ	γ	Gamma	Δ	δ	Delta
Ε	ε	Epsilon	Ζ	ζ	Zeta
Η	η	Eta	Θ	θ	Theta

Greek Alphabet: CONTINUED

Ι	ι	Iota	Κ	κ	Kappa
Λ	λ	Lambda	Μ	μ	Mu
Ν	ν	Nu	Ξ	ξ	Xi
Ο	ο	Omicron	Π	π	Pi
Ρ	ρ	Rho	Σ	σ ς	Sigma
Τ	τ	Tau	Υ	υ	Upsilon
Φ	φ	Phi	Χ	χ	Chi
Ψ	ψ	Psi	Ω	ω	Omega

αβγδεζηθικλμνξοπρσ
τυφχψως
ΑΒΓΔΕΖΗΘΙΚΛΜΝΞ
ΟΠΡΣΤΥΦΧΨΩ

αβγδεζηθικλμνξο
προστυφχψως ΑΒΓ
ΔΕΖΗΘΙΚΛΜΝΞ
ΟΠΡΣΤΥΦΧΨΩ

Greek Circumflex: an accent used in the Greek language.

⌒

Greek Cross: an ecclesiastical symbol in which the arms are of equal length and cross at their respective centres.

+

Grotesque: a style of sanserif type, generally of medium or heavy face.

Annonce Grotesque

Grotesque No. 6

GROTESQUE NO. 7

Grotesque No. 8

Grotesque No. 9

Grotesque No. 10

GROTESQUE No. 12

Grotesque No. 18

Inserat Grotesk

Groundline: a cameo letter appearing on black ground relieved with light vertical lines; also known as Cameo Lined.

GILL CAMEO RULED

Groundwork: ornaments or border elements capable of being arranged to give uniform and, generally, light-toned ground patterns as used on cheques, receipts, etc.; obtainable in a great variety of designs.

Groundwork: CONTINUED

Guillemets: a special form of quotation marks, used particularly in French; see also Quotation marks.

« » « » « » « » « » « » « »

« » « » « » « » « »

«Lune»

H

H: the eighth letter of the English alphabet.

Hh Hh *Hh* Hh

Hafnium: a metallic element. (Hf)

Hail: see Shower.

Hair Line: the curved neck or line connecting the main strokes; also known as arc of stem.

Hair-Line Letter: see Skeleton.

Hair-Line Rule: see Fine face rule.

Hair-Line Serif: one very fine and small, as in Bodoni, etc.

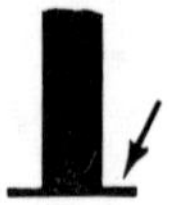

Half-Tone: a type-face of stippled effect.

HALF TONE NO. 1

HALF TONE NO. 2

Half Uncials: small letters of the alphabet, evolved about the sixth century.

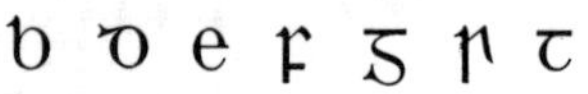

Halo: see Corona[1].

Hand: see Index.

Handletter: a type design of free lines, suggestive of hand production.

Freehand Series

Hand Tooled: a medium weight of type, relieved with a thin white line.

Cloister Cursive Handtooled

Goudy Handtooled

Hanging: the name sometimes given to old style figures (q.v.).

Harp: a musical instrument.

Haze: a meteorological symbol. ∞

He: see Hebrew alphabet.

Head: the apex of the type character.

→B V←

Head Piece: an ornamental element placed at the beginning of chapters in books.

Head Piece: CONTINUED

Heart[1]**:** an ornament in the shape of a heart.

Heart[2]**:** see Card pips.

Heavy: a significant thickness of stroke in a type face, as in Bodoni Heavy, etc.

BODONI HEAVY

CASLON OLD FACE HEAVY

Radiant Heavy

Tempo Heavy

Hebe: see Asteroid.

Hebrew Alphabet: consists of 23 letters and 13 points or accents; there is no differentiation of capitals and lower-case. Hebrew is read from right to left.

א Aleph	ב Beth	ג Gimel	ד Daleth
ה He	ו Vau	ז Zain	ח Cheth
ט Teth	י Jod	כ Caph	ל Lamed
מ Mem	נ Nun	ס Samech	ע Ain
פ Pe	צ Tzade	ק Koph	ר Resh
שׁ Shin	שׂ Sin	ת Tau	

Final letters

ך Caph ם Mem ן Nun ף Pe ץ Tzade

Broad letters

ﬡ Aleph ﬣ He ﬥ Lamed ﬦ Mem ﬨ Tau

Helium: a gaseous element. (He)

Hermaphrodite: a natural history symbol. ⚥ or ☿

Herschel: see Uranus.

Hexagon: a six-sided figure. ⬡

Hieroglyph: sacred or mysterious symbolic characters, particularly those used by the ancient Egyptians.

Hilite: a bold type face with thin white line relief.

Cooper Hilite

Historian: a symbol used to indicate historian in directories, in which composition space and time must be saved.

Hoar Frost: see Frost.

Holly Border: that designed as holly leaves and berries; obtainable for one or two-colour printing.

for two-colour printing

Holmium: a rare-earth element. (Ho)

Hook Serif: that which is bracketed or hooked to the main stem.

Horizontal Lines: sets of lines, particularly as equalization marks or summation rules.

=   ══════

Horse Power: a symbol used in engineering, electricity, etc.

HP

Hungarian Accents: those used in the Hungarian (Magyar) language.

áéíóöőúüű ÁÉÍÓÖŐÚÜŰ

Hybrid: a botanical symbol. ×

Hydrogen: a chemical substance. (H)

Hydrographic Signs: those used in marking of anchorages, etc.

 etc.

Hyphen: a punctuation mark used for connecting words, indicating divisions, etc.

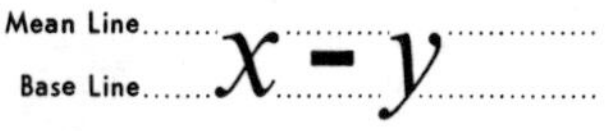

I

I: the ninth letter of the English alphabet.

Ii Ii *Ii* Ii

Ice: meteorological symbols, varying according to particular kind.

grains △ needles ↔

Icelandic Accents: the acute, the diaeresis, and (on old forms of o) reversed cedilla are used.

áðéíóöþúý ÁÐÉÍÓÖÞÚÝ

Icelandic D: a special symbol to indicate the sound approximately of th in that (English equivalent).

ð Ð

Icelandic P: a special symbol to indicate the sound approximately of th in thin (English equivalent).

þ Þ

Identical: see Congruence.

Ideographs: conventional symbols used to express some idea or name.

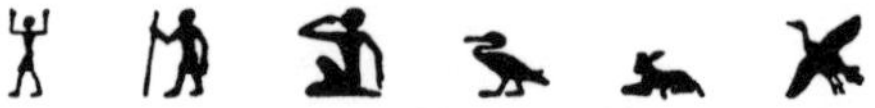

Illustrations: graphic images accepted as 'stock' representations of given objects.

Illustrations: CONTINUED

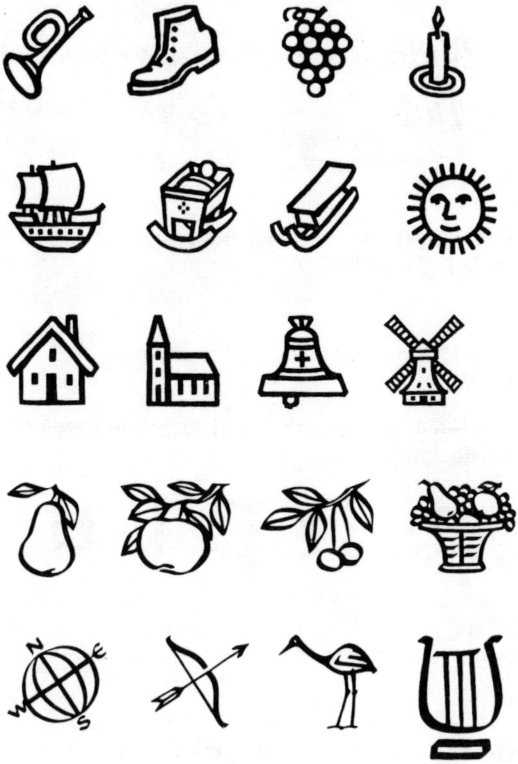

Implied By: a mathematical symbol. $\subset$

Implies: a mathematical symbol. $\supset$

Improper Fractions: those in which the numerator is greater than the denominator.

$$\frac{13}{3} \quad \frac{21}{4}$$

Inch: a symbol expressing inch or inches. ″

Inclined: lying at angle to the right (or left), as italic and script letters.

Bodoni Italic   *Invitation Script*   Pen Print

Inclined Parallels: fine parallel sloping lines used in chemical formulae.

Inclined Serif: one at angle, and commonly seen on various type designs.

m n p r u

Increase: see Crescendo.

Increment: a mathematical symbol. Δ

Incumbent: see Cotyledon.

Indefinite: see Infinity.

Index[1]: an indicator in the form of a pointing finger; also called fist, hand or pointer.

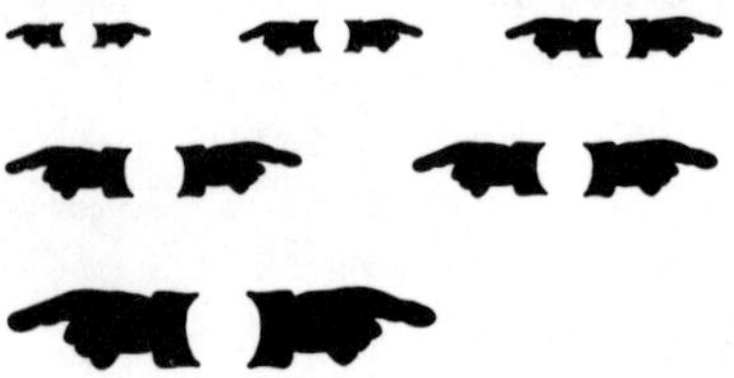

Index[1]**:** CONTINUED

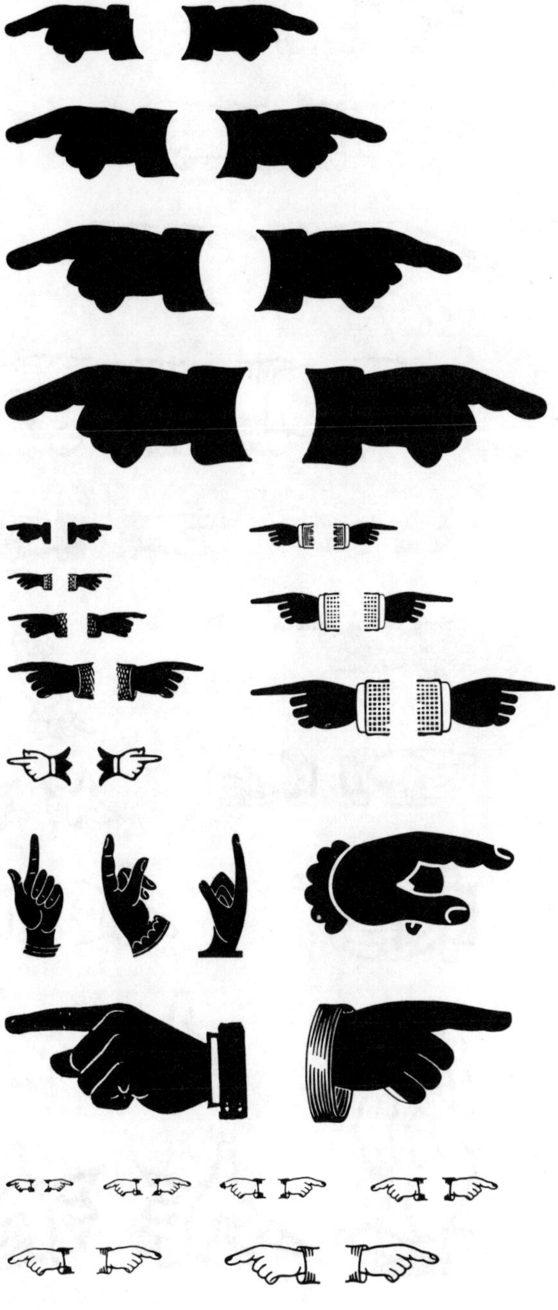

Index[1]**: CONTINUED**

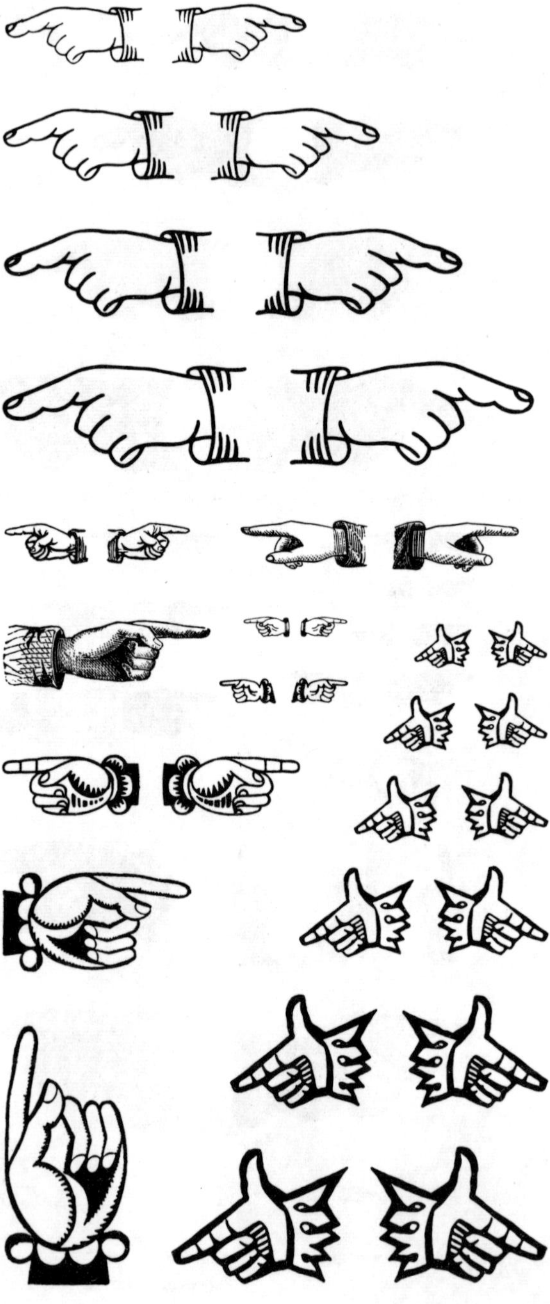

Index²: see Superior figures/letters.

Indium: a metallic element. (In)

Inequality: a mathematical symbol. $\neq$

Inferior Figures: those of about one-half the size of the body upon which they are positioned at the base of the shoulder; also known in algebra as suffixes.

$H_{1234567890}$

Inferior Letters: letters cast in the same manner as Inferior figures.

$H_{abcdefghijklmnopqrstuvwxyz}$

$H_{ABCDEFGHIJKLMNOPQRSTUVWXYZ}$

Infinity: a mathematical symbol; indicates countless or indefinite number.

∞

Initial Blanks: figured designs cast on pierced bodies for the insertion of any desired initial letter.

Initial Blanks: CONTINUED

Initial Letters: those used for the opening of chapters, etc., generally titling of a definite number of lines deep; made in many designs.

Initial Letters: CONTINUED

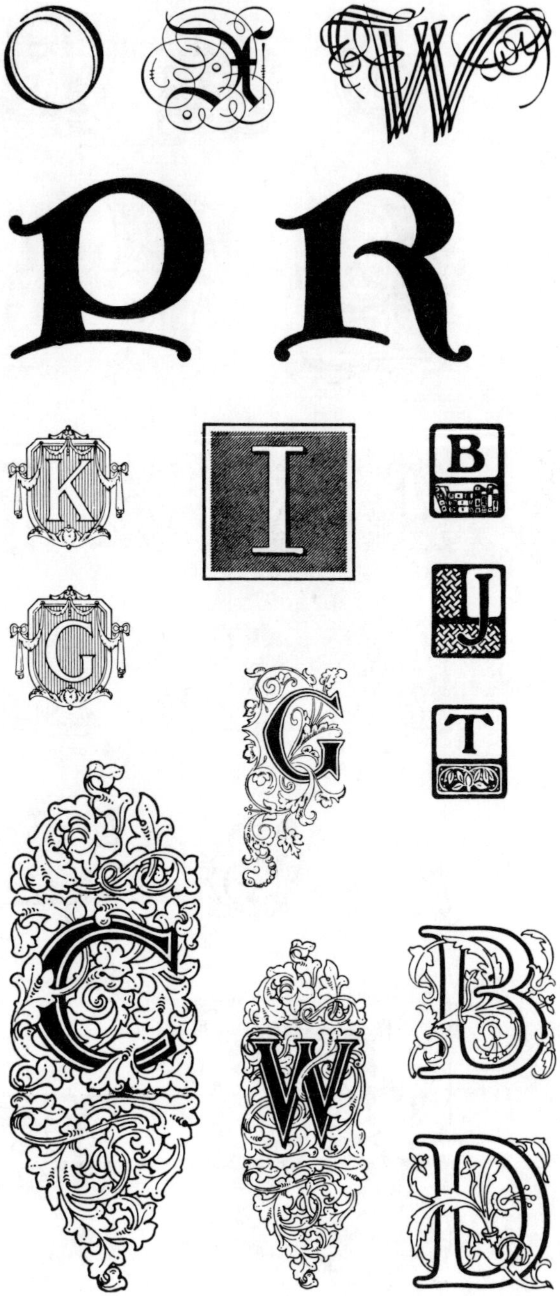

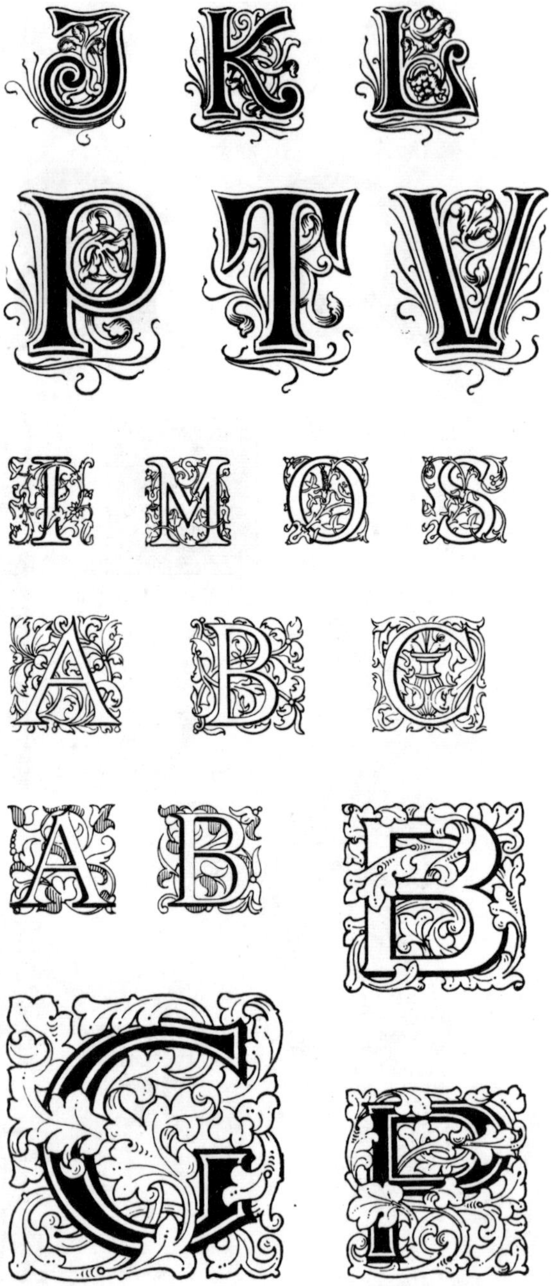

Initial Letters: CONTINUED

Inline (or Inlined): generally, a bold type relieved with a fine white line.

Cheltenham Inline

EGMONT INLINE

Granby Inlined

NEULAND INLINE

NOBEL INLINE

Inscribed: similar to Inline (q.v.).

Integration: a mathematical symbol.

Interchangeable: type faces in various sizes (but of the same design) cast upon a given depth of body; when set in one line they automatically align; also called lining, self-aligning or combination types.

6 point THE THE THE THE ·Plate Gothic

12 point THE THE THE THE

18 point THE THE THE

24 point THE THE

Interlocking Script: inclined imitation handwriting, the body of which is rhomboid and shaped so that each piece fits into and is held by the next.

International Copyright: see Unesco Copyright.

Interrogation, Mark of: see Question.

Inverted Circumflex: an accent used (e.g. in Czech) on certain letters.

ˇ (Ď Ě)

Inverted Commas: see Quotation marks.

Iodine: a chemical element. (I)

Iota: see Greek alphabet.

Iridium: a metallic element. (Ir)

Iris: see Asteroid.

Irish: see Gaelic.

Iron: a metallic element; takes its symbol from the Latin word Ferrum.

(Fe)

Italian: see Venetian.

Italian Accents: the acute and circumflex are used.

àèìîòù ÀÈÌÎÒÙ

Italic: a sloping form of letter; first used by **Aldus** Manutius (1501).

Blado

abcdefghijklmnopqrstuvwxyz

ABCDEFGHIJKLMN

OPQRSTUVWXYZ

Bembo

abcdefghijklmnopqrstuvwxyz

ABCDEFGHIJKLMNOPQRS

TUVWXYZ

Garamond

abcdefghijklmnopqrstuvwxyz

ABCDEFGHIJKLMNOPQ

RSTUVWXYZ

Caslon Old Face

abcdefghijklmnopqrstuvwxyz

ABCDEFGHIJKLMNOPQR

STUVWXYZ

Baskerville

abcdefghijklmnopqrstuvwxyz

ABCDEFGHIJKLMNOPQRST

UVWXYZ

Italic: CONTINUED

Bodoni

abcdefghijklmnopqrstuvwxyz
ABCDEFGHIJKLMNOPQRS
TUVWXYZ

Rockwell Medium

abcdefghijklmnopqrstu
vwxyz
ABCDEFGHIJKLMNOPQ
RSTUVWXYZ

Gill Sans Medium

abcdefghijklmnopqrstuvwxyz
ABCDEFGHIJKLMNOPQRSTUV
WXYZ

J

J: the tenth letter of the English alphabet.

Jj Jj *Jj* Jj

Jerusalem Cross: an ecclesiastical symbol the arms of which are terminated with a crossbar.

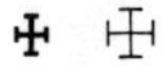

Jobbing Types: see Display types.

Joined: tied, actually as in ligatures, or apparently as in scripts.

ﬁ *Medium Script*

Juno: see Asteroid.

Jupiter: an astronomical symbol. ♃ ♃

K

K: the eleventh letter of the English alphabet.

Kk Kk Kk Kk

Kametz: see Masoretic points.

Kappa: see Greek alphabet.

Keltic Cross/Ornament: see Celtic.

Kern: the part of a letter overhanging its body.

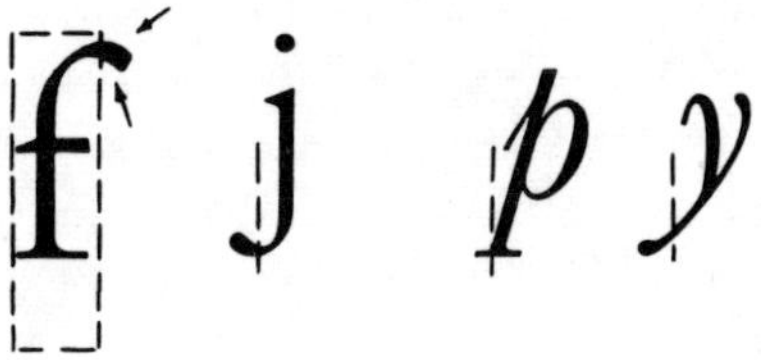

Kibbutz: see Masoretic points.

King: see Chess.

Knight[1]: a conventional symbol. 

Knight[2]: see Chess.

K.O.: an extraordinarily heavy weight of type.

Gill Kayo

Koph: see Hebrew alphabet.

Krypton: a rare gas. (Kr)

L

L: the twelfth letter of the English alphabet.

Ll Ll *Ll* Ll

Lambda: see Greek alphabet.

Lamed: see Hebrew alphabet.

Lanthanum: a rare-earth element. (La)

Large Face: a type cast to occupy more than the normal depth.

abcdefg ABC abcdefg ABC

small face large face

Latin: a style of type with strongly pronounced, wedge-shaped serifs.

LATIN

Latin Elongated **Bold Latin**

Bold Latin Condensed

Wide Latin

Latin Characters: those commonly used in England, in contradistinction to German, Greek, Russian, etc., characters; also known as Roman.

abcdefghijklmnopqrstuvwxyz
ABCDEFGHIJKLMNOPQ
RSTUVWXYZ

Latin Cross: an ecclesiastical symbol in which the short arm crosses the long above the latter's centre; also known as the crux immissa.

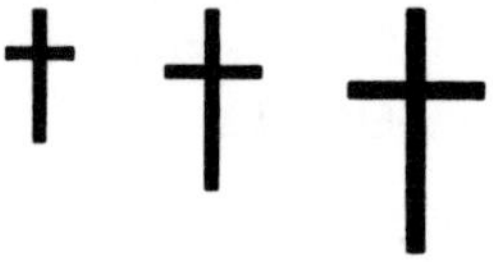

Latvian Accents: special forms, distinct from the standard accents, and including the long, inverted circumflex and stylized cedilla are used; also known as Lettish.

āčēģīķļņōŗšūž

ĀČĒĢĪĶĻŅŌŖŠŪŽ

Latvian G, K, L, N, R: see Latvian Accents.

Laurel[1]**:** a wreath of honour.

Laurel[2]**:** one of the elements of the Brooklyn border.

Laurel Leaves: a decorative and border element.

Lawyer: a symbol used to indicate lawyer in directories, in which composition space and time must be saved.

Lead: a metallic element; takes its symbol from the Latin word Plumbum.

(Pb)

Leader: an eye-guide, made in a variety of patterns.

.. 2-dot ....

... 3-dot ....

.... 4-dot ....

..... 5-dot ....

...... 6-dot ....

Lean: a rather condensed type face.

Juliana

abcdefghijklmnopqrstuvwxyz

ABCDEFGHIJKLMNOPQRSTUVWXYZ

Lectern: an ornament in the shape of a reading desk; one of the elements of the Brooklyn border.

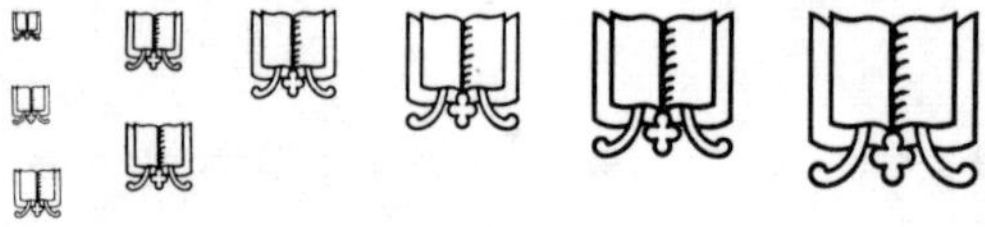

Leek: the national emblem of Wales.

Leger Lines: lines additional to the musical stave above or below which they are placed.

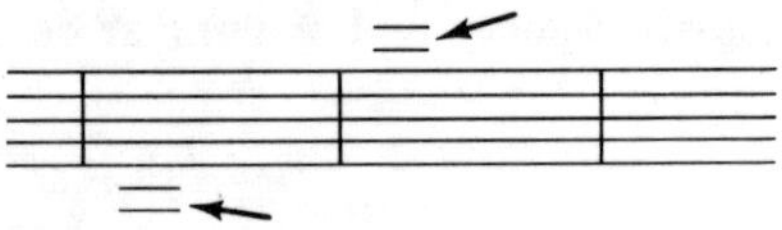

Lenis: see Breathings.

Leo: see Zodiac, Signs of.

Less: a mathematical symbol. $<$

Less or Greater: a mathematical symbol. $\lessgtr$

Less Than or Equal to: a mathematical symbol. $\leqq$ or $\leqslant$

Lettish: see Latvian Accents.

Libra[1]: see Pound.

Libra[2]: see Zodiac, Signs of.

Ligatures: bound or tied letters; those joined for expediency or ornament (see also Diphthong; Logotype).

fi ff fl ffi ffl

fi ff fl ffi ffl fr

ß ÿ fb fh fk fj ct qu st

ft ß ch ck

as is us et ct st

sp gg gy ta ll tt nt

ch ck k k

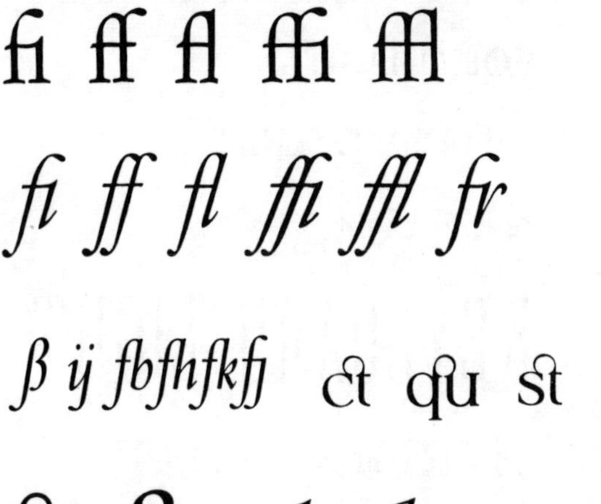

Light: a type design rather thinner in face than the standard.

Albertus Light

Bernhard Gothic Light

CARTOON LIGHT

CONSORT LIGHT

COPPERPLATE GOTHIC LIGHT

FOLIO LIGHT

GILL SANS LIGHT

Kabel Light

KEYBOARD LIGHT

LARGO LIGHT

Mercury Light   PEIGNOT LIGHT

Schadow Antiqua light

Stymie Light

Vogue Light

Lighthouse: a cartographical symbol. *

Lightning: a meteorological symbol. 

Lightning Flashes: zig-zag lines conventionally associated with drawings of flashes of lightning.

Light Refreshments: see Buffet car.

Line[1]: the standard against which type alignment is measured.

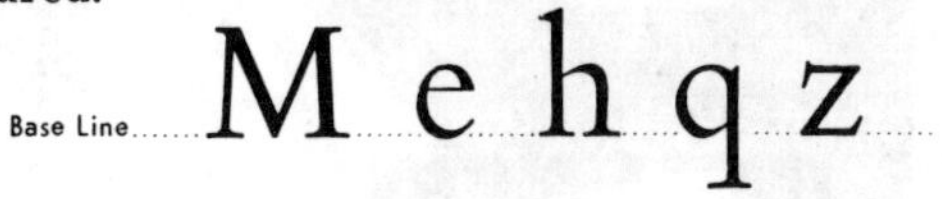

Line[2]: see Rule.

Linear Rule: see Milled rule.

Line Dash: see Pen dash.

Line Notes: those in music cast with a line through them.

Lines Deep: the measuring standard for the body depth of poster letters; 8 line letter=eight lines of 12 pt.

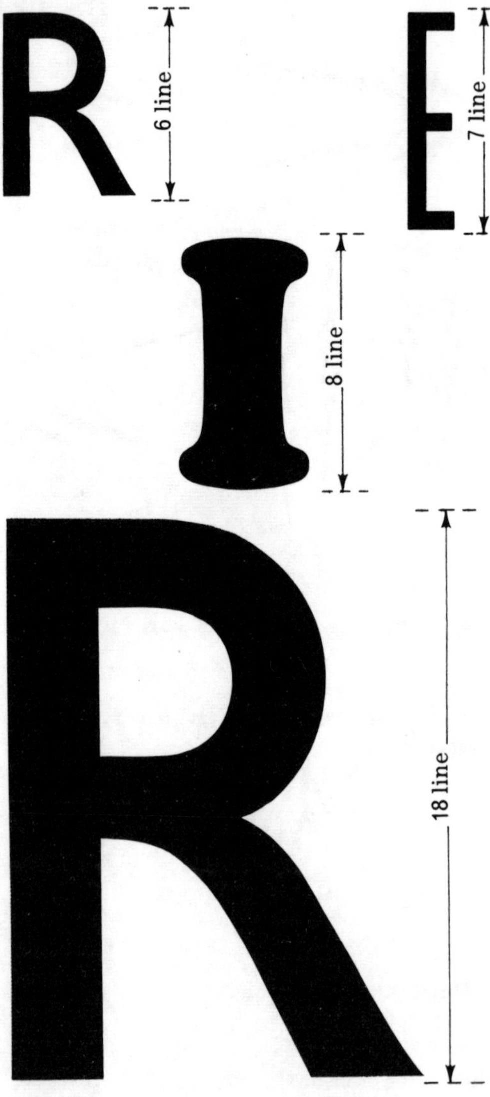

Line to Back: the distance from the base line of the type to the back of the shank.

Line to Front: the distance from the base line of the type to the front of the shank.

Lining Figures: arabic figures, cast on nut quad body, of equal height, ranging at foot and head; also called capital, modern, newspaper or tall figures (see also Old Style figures).

1 2 3 4 5 6 7 8 9 0

Lining Type: see Interchangeable.

Link[1]: the line joining the upper and lower parts of the lower case g.

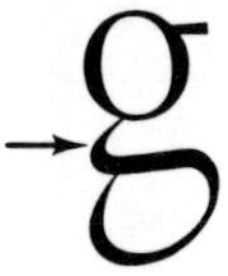

Link[2]: a connecting line, especially of some script letters.

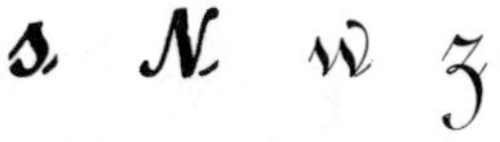

Linked Letters: see Logotype.

Lips: the unserifed ends of certain round letters.

C← c e

Lira: a symbol used in Italian currency; plural=lire.

₤

Literary Work: a symbol used to indicate a book, etc., in directories, in which composition space and time must be saved.

Lithium: a metallic element. (Li)

Lithuanian Accents: special forms are used, including reversed cedilla, inverted circumflex, long and dotted accents.

ąčėęįšūųž ĄČĖĘĮŠŪŲŽ

Lithuanian A, E, I, U: see Lithuanian Accents.

Lobe: the bowl (q.v.) of a character.

Locomotive: see Train.

Logotype: several letters or a word cast on one body (see also Diphthong: Ligature).

ST ND RD TH *St* **pr qt**

Pi *Th* *Vi* **yd dz**

Logotype: CONTINUED

Mr st th o' s'

Dr. to R.S.V.P. ent heit

The Ltd. of The If Of Off

E J T SMALL CANS LARGE CANS POISON
A A I
C R N 8-OZ. CANS 1-LB. CANS
H S S

Chelsea Everton Fulham

Coca-Cola DUMBARTON

CINEMASCOPE SUN

OCTOBER

Long Accent: a horizontal line over a letter; also called the macron or straight accent.

ā ē ī ō ū

Long Ascenders: unusually tall extruders.

b d f h k l

Long Descenders: extra-long tails to letters.

Long Letters: those that occupy the entire depth of body.

 etc.

Long S: an obsolete form of lower-case s.

Loop[1]: an oval part of a letter in contradistinction to the bowl.

Loop[2]: a line crossing a main stem and thus forming an oval shape, as in many script characters.

Loose Accents: see Accents, floating.

Lorraine, Cross of: a cross composed of an upper and a lower horizontal line on a single vertical.

Lower Case: the minuscules of the fount, of various heights and forms.

abcdefghijklmnopqrstuvwxyz

abcdefghijklmnopqrstuvwxyz

abcdefghijklmnopqrstuvwxyz

abcdefghijklmnopqrstu
vwxyz

abcdefghijklmnopqrstuvwxyz

abcdefghijklmnopqrstuvwxyz

abcdefghijklmnop
qrstuvwxyz

abcdefghijklmnopqrstu
vwxyz

abcdefghijklmnopqrstuvwxyz

*abcdefghijklmnopqrst
uvwxyz*

abcdefghijklmnopqrs
tuvwxyz

abcdefghijklmnopqrstuvwxyz

Lower Case: CONTINUED

abcdefghijklmnopqrstu
vwxyz

abcdefghijklmnopqrstuv
wxyz

abcdefghijklmnopqrstuvwxyz

abcdefghijklmnopqrstuvwxyz

abcdefghijklmnopqrst
uvwxyz

abcdefghijklmnopqrst
uvwxyz

abcdefghijklmnopqrstuvwxyz

abcdefghijklmnopqrst
uvwxyz

abcdefghijklmnopqrst
uvwxyz

abcdefghijklmnopqrst
uvwxyz

abcdefghijklmnopqrstuvwxyz

Lozenge: a diamond-shaped parallelogram. ◇

Lug: see Cat's ear.

Lugged Sorts: those cast with projections for supporting kerns; they necessitate the use of specially cast letters on smaller bodies.

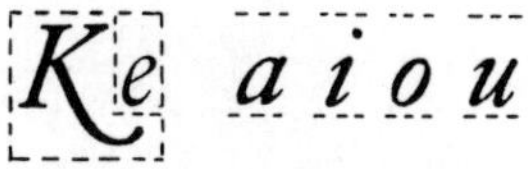

Lunar: see Corona[1].

Lunation: see Moon.

Lutetium: a rare-earth element. (Lu)

Lyre: a harp-like instrument; a symbol also used in combination or multiples as borders or ornaments.

M

M: the thirteenth letter of the English alphabet.

Mm Mm Mm Mm

Macron: see Long accent.

Magnesium: a metallic element. (Mg)

Magyar: see Hungarian Accents.

Magyar O, U: see Hungarian Accents.

Mail Coach: a symbol used in some continental timetables to indicate post wagon.

Majority: see Greater than.

Majuscules: see Capitals.

Male: a botanical or zoological symbol. ♂

Maltese Accents: those used in the language of Malta.

âċġħìṅ ÂĊĠHÌṄ

Maltese Cross: an ecclesiastical symbol of special design; also known as the eight-pointed or square cross.

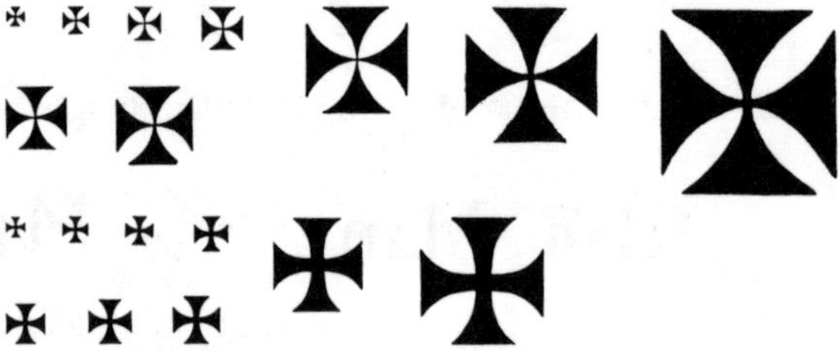

Maltese H: a double-barred capital and cross-stemmed lower-case letter.

Ħ ħ

Manganese: a metallic element. Ⓜn

Manx Cross: a religious symbol consisting of a cross surrounded by a circle; also known as Wheel cross.

⊕

Mappik: see Hebrew alphabet.

Mark: a unit of German currency. ℳ

Mars: an astronomical symbol. ♂

Masonic Signs: stylized symbols relating to Freemasonry.

Masoretic Points: marks used in Hebrew as vowel sounds; their position alone is enough to indicate differences.

cholem	וֹ	pathach	אַ
kametz	אָ	segol	אֶ
kametz chatuph	אָ	sheva	בְ
kibbutz	בֻ	shurek	וּ
short chirek	אִ	tzeri	אֵ
long chirek	יִ		

Mathematical Signs: see under individual names, e.g. Addition, Division, etc.

Maximum Gauge: the depth of face of the longest character in the fount.

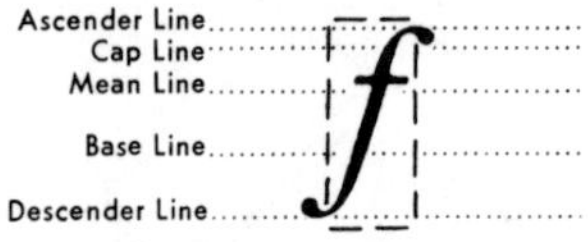

Mean Line: the imaginary line running along the tops of the short letters.

Medals: coinlike symbols emblematic of rewards.

Medium: the weight or colour of a type face that may be regarded as the standard.

Cheltenham Medium

City Medium

Egizio Medium

EGMONT MEDIUM

HELVETICA MEDIUM

OFFENBACH MEDIUM

Post Roman Medium

POST TITLE MEDIUM

Signal Medium Walbaum Medium

Medium Face Rule: that with a face of approximately ½ pt. thickness.

Mem: see Hebrew alphabet.

Mercury[1]: an astronomical symbol. ☿

Mercury[2]: a liquid metal; takes its symbol from the Greek-Latin word Hydrargyrum. (Hg)

Mercury[3]: see Caduceus.

Metal Rule: a horizontal line cut centrally on some recognized body depth in the type metal alloy; normally made in sizes of from one to four ems; also called the dash.

Meteorological Symbols: see under individual names, e.g. Aurora, Rime, etc.

Mezzo-Forte: a symbol used in music. *mf*

Middle Serif: one appearing over the centre stroke of the w.

Milled Rule: that consisting of short, closely spaced lines; also known as Linear, Simplex, or Utility rule.

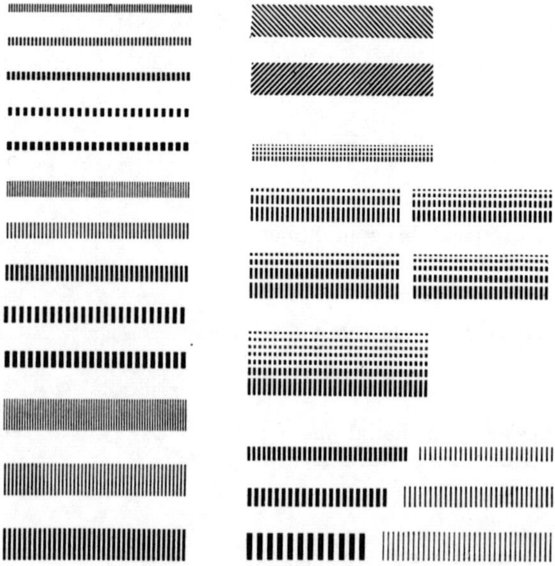

Millimetre: a measurement in the metric system.

m/m m/m m/m m/m

Million: one thousand thousands in Roman numeration.

$\overline{\mathrm{M}}$

Miner: a symbol used to indicate miner in directories, in which composition space and time must be saved.

Mineralogist: a symbol used to indicate mineralogist in directories, in which composition space and time must be saved. 

Minim[1]: a medical symbol.  or ♏

Minim[2]: a white, stemmed note in music, one-half the value of the semi-breve.

Minority: see Less than.

Minus: the sign of subtraction.

– – – – – – —
– – – – – –

Minuscules: see Lower-case.

Minus or Plus: a mathematical symbol. ∓ ∓ ∓ ∓

Minute: the symbol indicating minute. ′

Mirage: a meteorological symbol. ⋈

Mist: a meteorological symbol.

light $\equiv^{0}$ heavy $\equiv^{2}$

Mitre: an ecclesiastical hat.

archbishop    bishop 

Mitred Rule: printer's rule of which the ends are cut at angle to allow of neat joining.

 thus 

Mix: a medical symbol. M̶

Modelling: the characteristic emphasis of the strokes forming the round letters; also known as bias, shading, stress.

backward O   italic *O*

vertical O

Modern: type faces in which the difference between thick and thin strokes is strongly marked; and with sharp, often hair-line, non-bracketed serifs, giving a brilliant, dazzling letter form, as in the specimens below.

WALBAUM

abcdefghijklmnop
qrstuvwxyz ABCD
EFGHIJKLMNOPQ
RSTUVWXYZ

BODONI 135

Craw Modern

ELONGATED ROMAN

Modern No. 20

Modern Figures: see Lining figures.

Modulus: a mathematical symbol. μ or $|$

Molybdenum: a metallic element. Ⓜo

Monaural: a special symbol to indicate basic sound in music. Ⓜ

Monetary Symbols: see under individual names, e.g. Pound, Dollar, Cent, etc.

Monocarp: a plant that bears fruit once.

monocarpic annual ①

monocarpic biennial ②

hardy monocarp (∞)

Monograms: founts by which any desired combination of initials may be brought together.

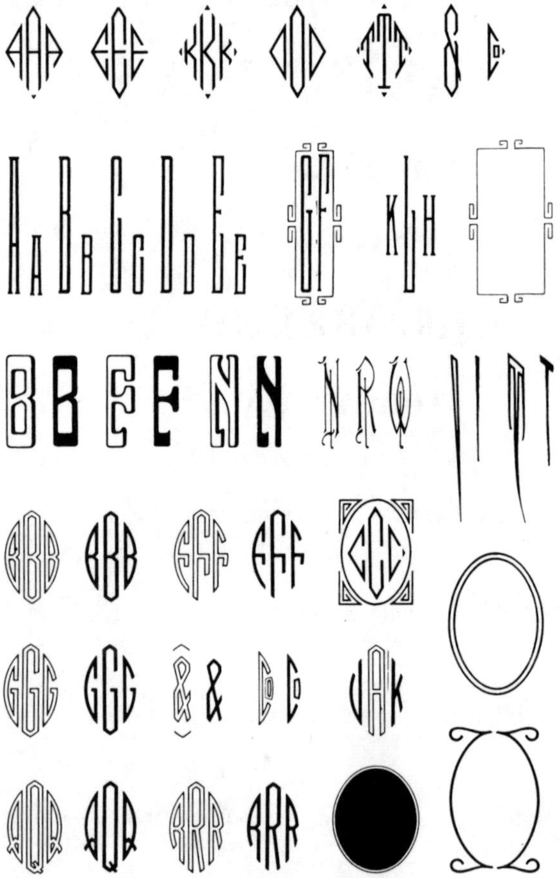

Moon: an astronomical symbol.

The four lunations:

new	first quarter	full	last quarter

Mordent: a symbol used in music to indicate trill with upper or lower note.

upper  lower  etc.

Morse: symbols used to designate the letters of the alphabet as given by the Morse code.

A	• —	E	•
B	— • • •	F	• • — •
C	— • — •	G	— — •
D	— • •	H	• • • •

Morse: CONTINUED

I	• •	R	• — •
J	• — — —	S	• • •
K	— • —	T	—
L	• — • •	U	• • —
M	— —	V	• • • —
N	— •	W	• — —
O	— — —	X	— • • —
P	• — — •	Y	— • — —
Q	— — • —	Z	— — • •

1	• — — — —
2	• • — — —
3	• • • — —
4	• • • • —
5	• • • • •
6	— • • • •
7	— — • • •
8	— — — • •
9	— — — — •
0	— — — — —

Mu: see Greek alphabet.

Multiplication: the sign of multiplying.

× × × × × × ×

× × × × × ×

Musician: a symbol used to indicate musician in directories, in which composition space and time must be saved.

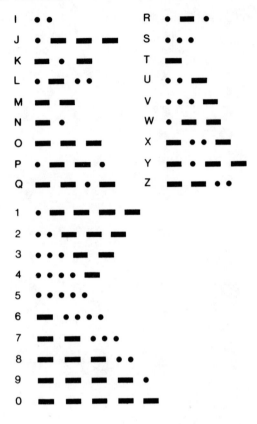

Music Signs: see under individual names, e.g. Breve, Crotchet, etc.

Music Type: that consisting of single pieces, such as note-heads, lines, bars, etc., put together to form complete musical sense.

Mutton Rule: see Em rule.

Mutuality: a mathematical symbol implying mutual implication. $\leftrightarrow$

Mythologist: a symbol used to indicate mythologist in directories, in which composition space and time must be saved.

N

N: the fourteenth letter of the English alphabet.

𝔑𝔫 Nn *Nn* Nn

Nabla: a mathematical symbol. ∇

Naissance: a symbol used to indicate birth in directories, in which composition space and time must be saved.

∗ or ★

Narrow: a type having lesser width than normal.

NARROW GOTHIC TITLING

Narrow Sans Italic

Natural: a musical symbol. ♮

Nearly Equal to: a mathematical symbol. $\cong$

Negative: a mathematical or electrical symbol. —

Neodymium: a rare-earth element. (Nd)

Neon: a gaseous element. (Ne)

Neptune: an astronomical symbol. ♆ or Ψ

Neptunium: a transuranic radio-active element. (Np)

Newspaper Figures: see Lining figures.

Newspaper Fractions: see Combination fractions.

Nickel: a metallic element. (Ni)

Nine: the symbol for a nonuple quantity.

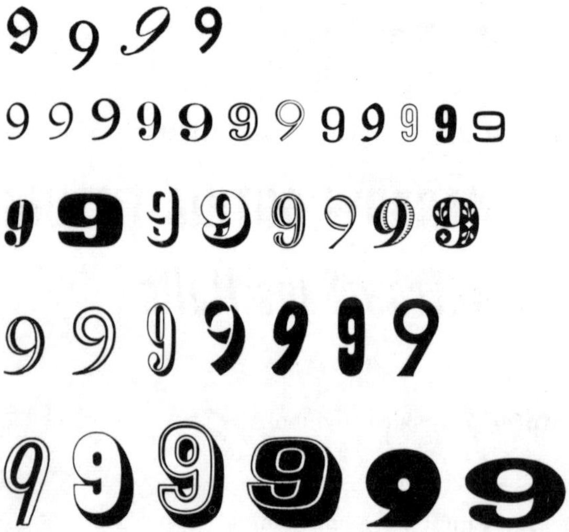

Niobium: a metallic element. Ⓝⓑ (Nb)

Niton: a former name for the element radon (q.v.).

Nitrogen: a gaseous element. Ⓝ

Node: an intersecting point, or bud-swelling.

ascending	descending
☊	☋
(Dragon's head)	(Dragon's tail)

Non-Congruence: a mathematical symbol expressing non-agreement between numbers.

$\not\equiv$

Non-Kerning: applicable to type characters which do not overhang the body.

Norwegian O: see Danish O.

Not Contains: a mathematical symbol. $\not\supset$

Note of Interrogation: see Question mark.

Not Equal: a mathematical symbol. $\neq$ or $\neq$

Not Greater: a mathematical symbol. $\ngtr$ or $\leqq$

Not Identical: see Non-congruence.

Not Less: a mathematical symbol. $\nless$ or $\geq$

Nought: see Nullo.

Nu: see Greek alphabet.

Nuller: the symbol of ditto or repetition. ״

Nullo: the nought or zero.

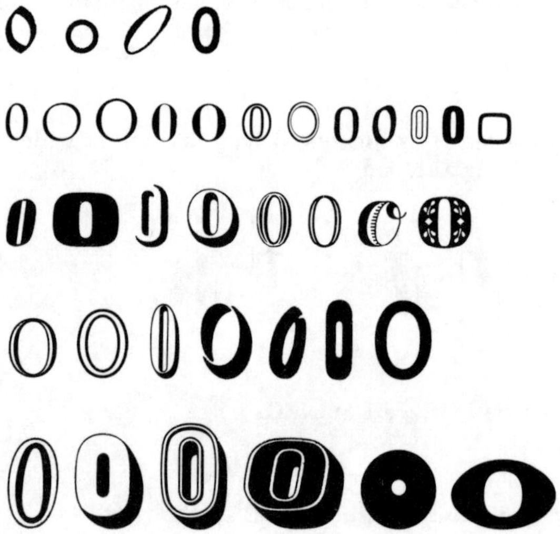

Number: a commercial symbol-contraction.

№ № N° N°

(used in America)

# # # # # # # #

Numbered Figures: those in which the value appears in words on the figure.

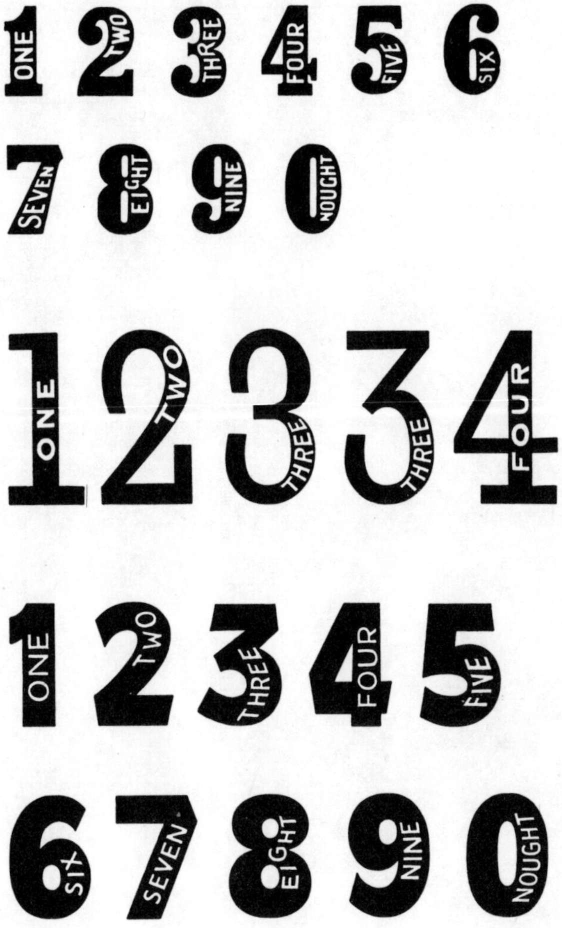

Numerals: see Lining figures; Old Style figures; Roman numerals.

Nun: see Hebrew alphabet.

Nut Quad Fractions: see Straight fractions.

O

O: the fifteenth letter of the English alphabet.

Oo Oo *Oo* Oo

Obelisk: see Dagger.

Obelus: see Dagger.

Oblique[1]: of italic design or slope.

Vogue Extra
Bold Oblique

Oblique[2]: see Separatrix.

Oblique Cross: see Crux decussata.

Œ: see Diphthong.

Officer: a symbol used to indicate officer in directories, in which composition space and time must be saved.

naval ƒ ⚓ military ƒ

Ohm: a symbol for the electrical unit of resistance. Ω

Old English: see Black letter.

Old Face: roman types designed after the models of the early sixteenth century; with fairly well-defined differences between thin and thick strokes, bracketed serifs, subtle gradation of 'colour', long ascenders and descenders. These letters themselves derive from the 1495 Aldine roman.

VAN DIJCK

abcdefghijklmnopqrstuv

wxyz ABCDEFGHIJKL

MNOPQRSTUVWXYZ

BEMBO

Poliphilus

Garamond

Granjon Old Face

Janson

CASLON OLD FACE

IMPRINT

Old Style: the name of a group of serifed type faces, having the general characteristics of Old Face but lighter in weight and with less strongly pronounced differences between thin and thick strokes; often with short descenders.

OLD STYLE

abcdefghijklmnopqrstuvwxyz

ABCDEFGHIJKLMNO

PQRSTUVWXYZ

Century Oldstyle

Light Oldstyle Series

OLD STYLE No. 2

OLD STYLE No. 4

Old Style No. 6

Old Style Figures: those supplied originally with old style founts and having no uniform alignment (see also Lining figures).

1 2 3 4 5 6 7 8 9 0

Old Style Fractions: see Diagonal fractions.

Omega: see Greek alphabet.

Omicron: see Greek alphabet.

Omission, Mark of: see Caret.

One: the symbol for unity.

Open: generally, an outline form of letter, though occasionally having some strokes very slightly thicker than others.

Bodoni Open

Howland Open

LE CHAMPLEVÉ

Lucian Open

Minster Black Open

OLD FACE OPEN

Open Bracket: a symbol sometimes used in mathematical statements.

[ ] [ ]

Open Note: see White note.

Open P: see Paragraph.

Open Quotation (mark): a specially designed symbol for beginning a quoted passage, in contradistinction to the inverted comma, and used either singly or as a pair.

Opposition: a symbol indicating that the position of heavenly bodies is diametrically opposed.

☍

Orders: offices or honours, or the badges relating thereto.

Ornamental Cross: an ecclesiastical symbol, the arms of which end with balls.

Ornamental Dash: that usually consisting of a short line with filigree decoration (see also Pen dash).

Ornamental Dash: CONTINUED

Ornamented Letters: see Fancy type faces.

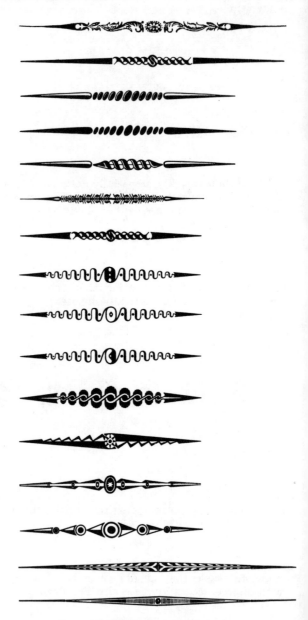

Ornaments: printing elements of decorative pattern, cast in many sizes and innumerable designs; capable of use alone or arranged as continuous lines, borders, etc.

Ornithologist: a symbol used to indicate ornithologist in directories, in which composition space and time must be saved.

Osmium: a metallic element. (Os)

Ounce: a medical symbol. ℥

Outline: the form of the type face indicated by simple lines, generally of uniform weight.

Advertisers
Gothic Outline

Outline: CONTINUED

Cheltenham Bold Outline

Contour

Tudor Black Outline

WHEDONS Gothic Outline

Windsor Outline

Ovals: lead or brass hollow shapes for the insertion of type matter; may be obtained in various patterns.

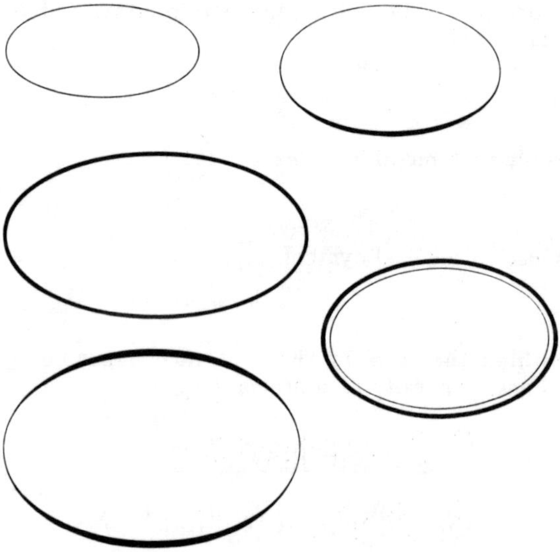

Ovals: CONTINUED

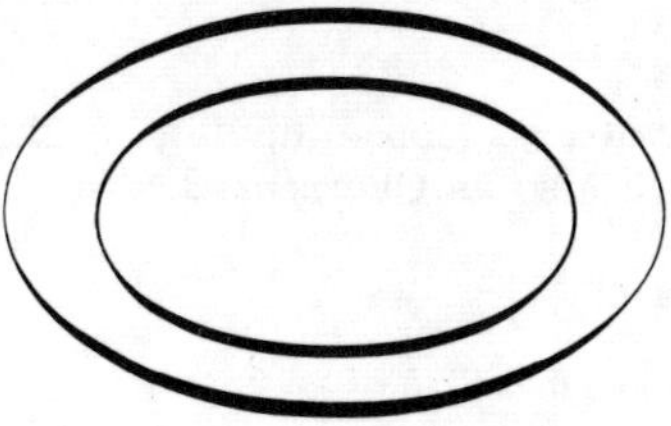

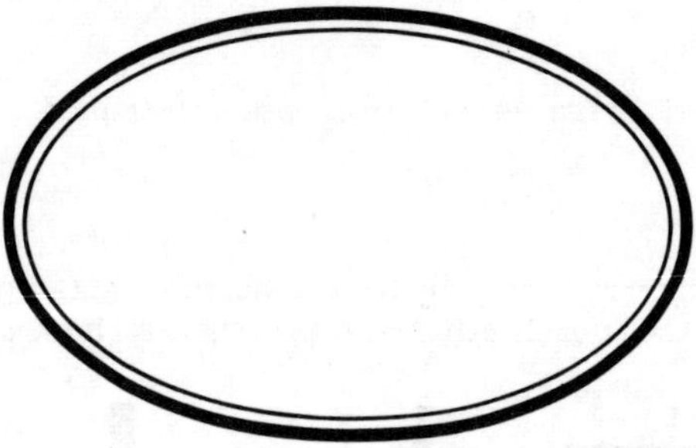

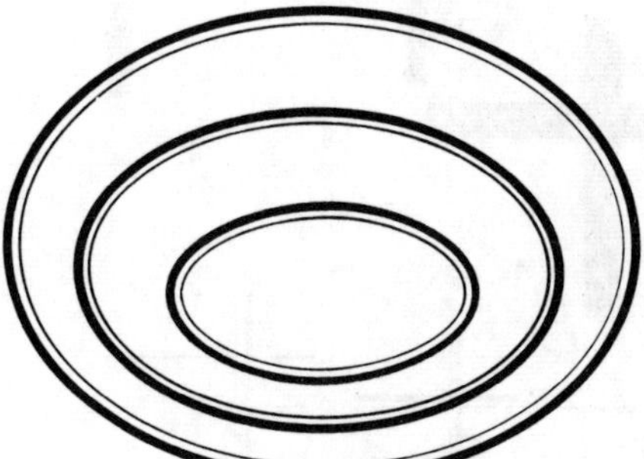

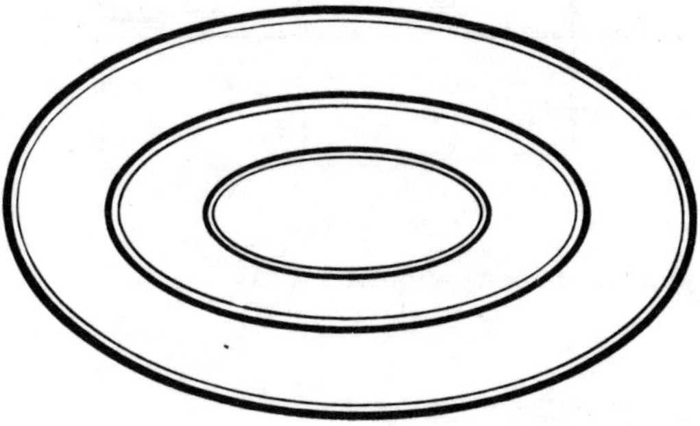

Overhang: see Kern.

Overlined Figures/Letters: those having a short line above them; known also as Overscored.

$\overline{1}\ \overline{2}\ \overline{3}\ \overline{4}\ \overline{5}\ \overline{6}\ \overline{7}\ \overline{8}\ \overline{9}\ \overline{0}$

$\overline{a}\ \overline{b}\ \overline{c}\ \overline{d}\ \overline{e}\ \overline{f}\ \overline{g}\ \overline{h}\ \overline{i}\ \overline{j}\ \overline{k}\ \overline{l}\ \overline{m}\ \overline{n}\ \overline{o}\ \overline{p}\ \overline{q}\ \overline{r}\ \overline{s}\ \overline{t}\ \overline{u}\ \overline{v}\ \overline{w}\ \overline{x}\ \overline{y}\ \overline{z}$

$\overline{A}\ \overline{B}\ \overline{C}\ \overline{D}\ \overline{E}\ \overline{F}\ \overline{G}\ \overline{H}\ \overline{I}\ \overline{J}\ \overline{K}\ \overline{L}\ \overline{M}\ \overline{N}\ \overline{O}\ \overline{P}\ \overline{Q}\ \overline{R}\ \overline{S}\ \overline{T}\ \overline{U}\ \overline{V}\ \overline{W}\ \overline{X}\ \overline{Y}\ \overline{Z}$

Overscored Figures/Letters: see Overlined figures/letters.

Oxford Corners: those in which the rules making up the border cross each other and protrude a short distance.

Oxygen: a gaseous element. Ⓞ

Oyin: see Hebrew alphabet.

P

P: the sixteenth letter of the English alphabet.

Pp Pp Pp Pp

Painter: a symbol used to indicate painter in directories, in which composition space and time must be saved.

Palæographical Signs: see Scribal Abbreviations.

Palladium: a metallic element. (Pd)

Pallas: see Asteroid.

Papal Cross: an ecclesiastical symbol having three cross-bars of different lengths; also known as the triple cross.

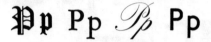

Paragraph: a symbol used to denote the beginning of paragraphs; also the sixth reference mark in bookwork; known as the blind, open or reversed P.

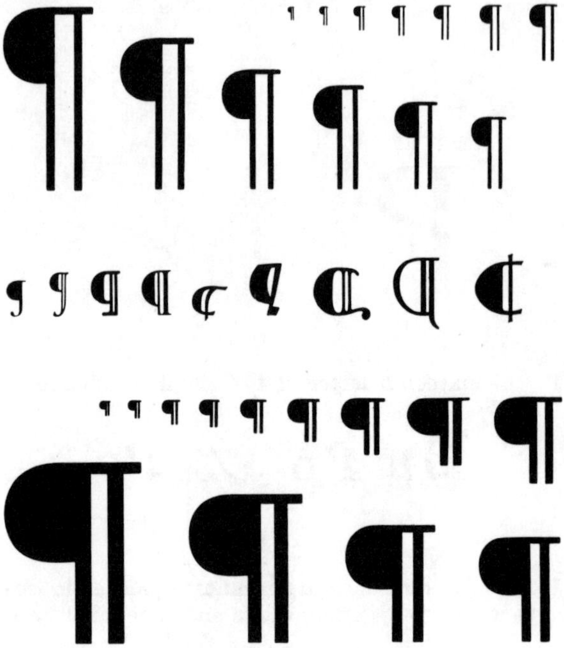

Parallel: the fifth bookwork reference mark.

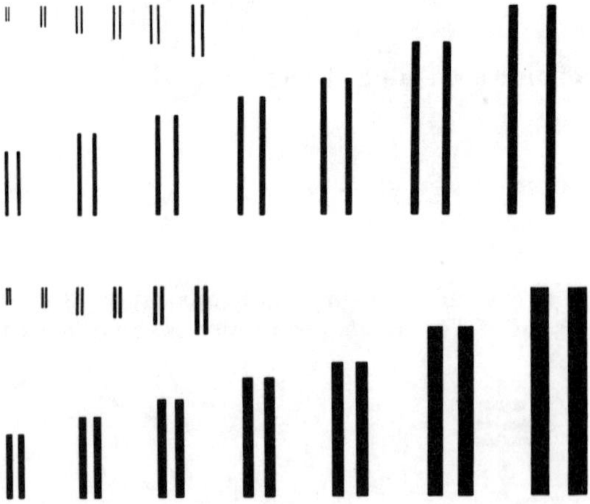

Parenthesis: punctuation marks used to enclose a phrase, etc.; sometimes called Round brackets (plural parentheses).

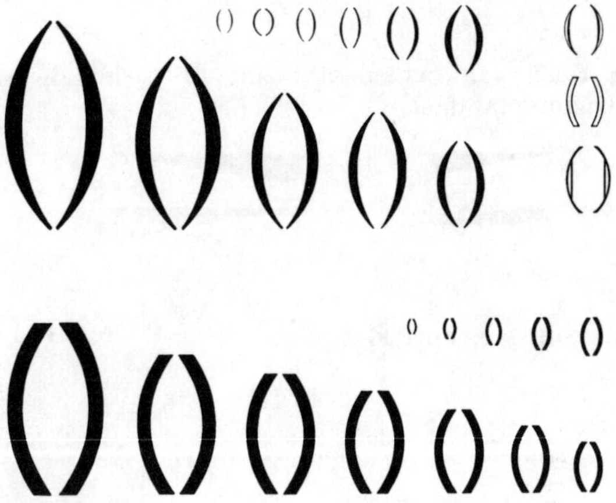

Pathach: see Masoretic points.

Patibulata: see St. Anthony's cross.

Patriarchal Cross: an ecclesiastical symbol having two bars; also known as the Archbishop's, Cardinal's or Double cross.

Pause: a symbol used in music to denote lengthening or cessation of sound; also known as Corona.

Pawn: see Chess.

Pe: see Hebrew alphabet.

Peculiars: extraneous sorts of any description.

@ ♂ « m/m © ☛ ℞ ϶ ′ ☺ √ etc.

Pen Dash: an ornamental line or terminal (see also Ornamental dash).

Pentagon: a five-sided figure. ⬠

Per: a commercial symbol = at or by.

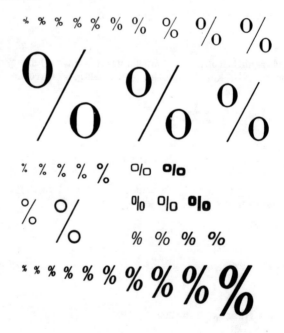

Per Cent (or Centum): a commercial symbol = by the hundred.

% % % % % % % % % %

% % %

% % % % % %/o %/o

% % %/o %/o %/o

% % % %

% % % % % % % % % %

Per Cent (or Centum): CONTINUED

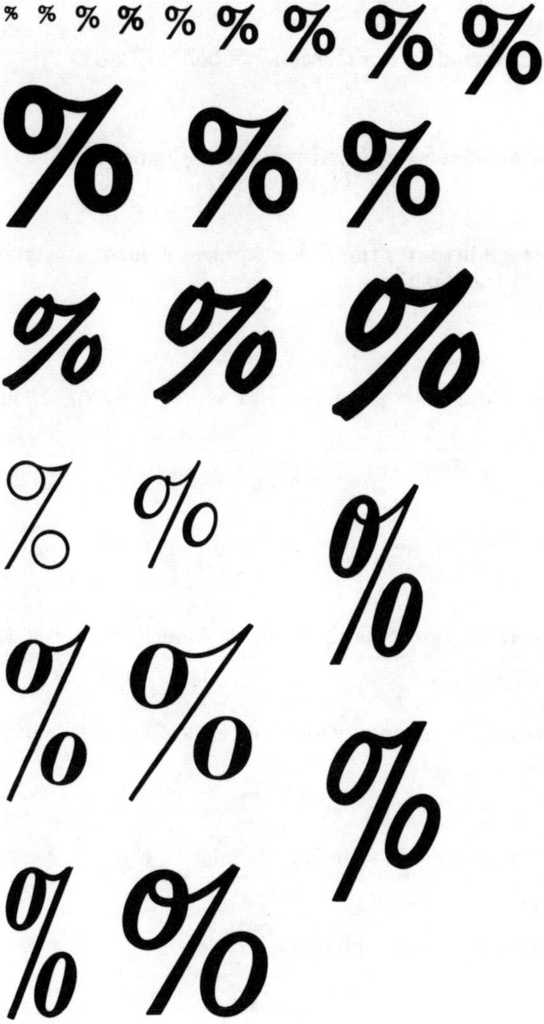

Perennial: a plant that lives for more than two years.

♃

Period: see Full point.

Per Mil(le): see Per thousand.

Per Myriad: a commercial symbol. ‱

Perpendicular[1]**:** a mathematical symbol. ⊥

Perpendicular[2]**:** the typographical symbol at right angles to the dash. |

Per Thousand: a commercial symbol = by the thousand. ‰

Peseta: a symbol used in Spanish currency. ₧

Peso: a symbol used in South American currencies. ₱

Pfennig: a monetary symbol (unit of German currency). ₰

Pharmacist: a dispensing chemist. ⚖

Phi: see Greek alphabet.

Philatelist: a symbol used to indicate philatelist in directories, in which composition space and time must be saved.

Philologist: a symbol used to indicate philologist in directories, in which composition space and time must be saved.

Philosopher: a symbol used to indicate philosopher in directories, in which composition space and time must be saved.

 or ⁂

Phonetic Alphabet: a collection of symbols designed to assist pronunciation of words in different languages; evolved by the International Phonetics Association.

a ɑ ɒ æ β c ç ɕ ɔ χ ɖ ð e ɛ ɟ g ɢ ɦ ħ ɥ i ɨ ɪ j ʃ ɬ ɭ ɮ

ɱ ɯ ɳ ɲ ŋ ɴ o ø ɵ ʊ œ ɸ q ʀ ʁ ɹ ɽ s ʂ ʃ ʈ θ u ʉ

v ʌ ʋ ɤ ɣ w x y ʎ ʏ z ʐ ʒ ʑ ʔ ʕ

Phosphorus: a non-metallic element. (P)

Physician: a symbol used to indicate physician in directories, in which composition space and time must be saved.

Physicist: a symbol used to indicate physicist in directories, in which composition space and time must be saved.

∩

Pi[1]**:** the ratio of the circumference to the diameter of a circle; 3.1416.

π

Pi[2]**:** see Greek alphabet.

Pianissimo: a direction in music (=very softly).

pp

Pianississimo: a direction in music (=as softly as possible).

Piano: a direction in music (=softly).

Picture: a symbol used to indicate painted picture in directories, in which composition space and time must be saved.

O ☞

Piece Brace/Bracket: see Brace; Bracket.

Pisces: see Zodiac, Signs of.

Pitman's Augmented Alphabet: that consisting of forty-three characters, based on the existing English alphabet (less q x) but with specialized signs for given sounds.

a	˙a	˙æ	˙au	b	c	˙ch
d	e	˙ɛɛ	f	g	h	i
˙ie	j	k	l	m	n	˙ŋ
o	˙œ	˙ɔi	˙ou	˙ω	˙ꞷ	p
r	s	˙ʃh	˙ʒ	˙ʒ	t	˙th
˙th	u	˙ue	v	w	˙wh	y
Z	children lern tω reɛd thrꞷ i.t.a.					

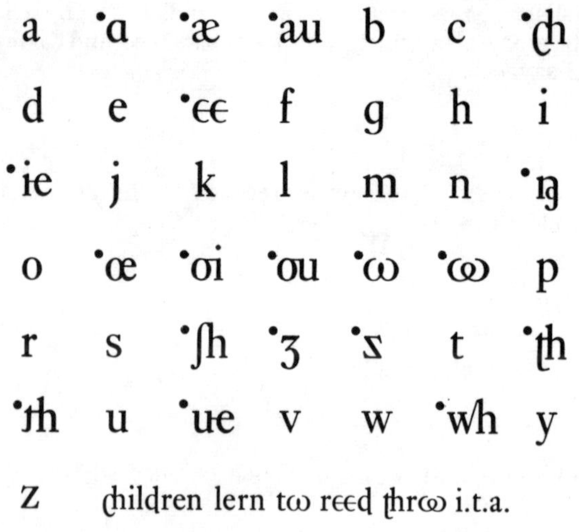

˙Augmented characters.

Plaid Border: see Tartan border.

Platinum: a metallic element. Ⓟ Pt

Playing Cards: representations of the various members of each card suit (see also Card pips).

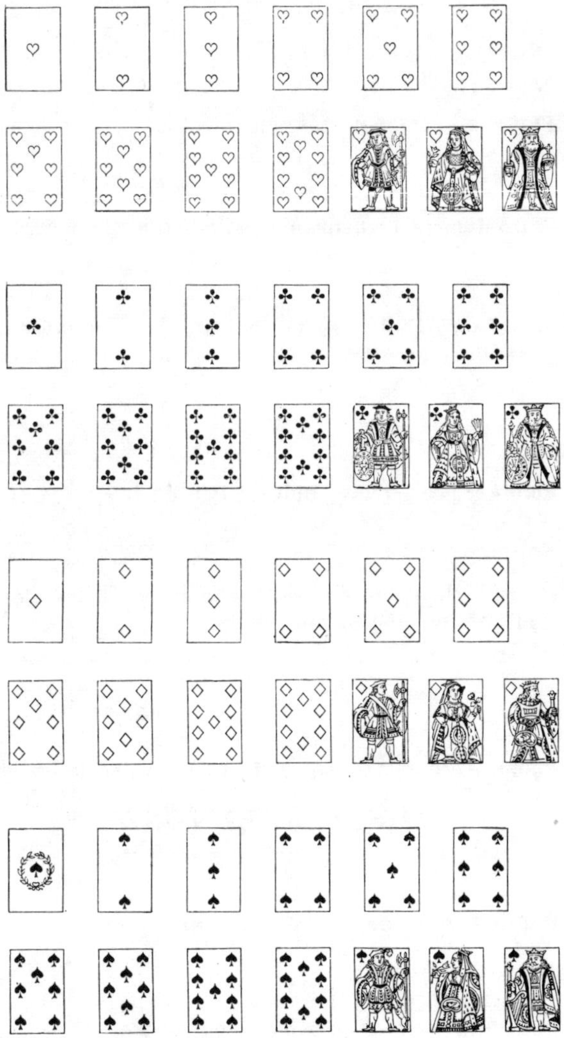

Plus: see Addition.

Plus or Minus: a combination of the signs for addition and subtraction.

± ± ± ± ± ±

± ± ± ± ± ±

± ± ± ±

Pluto: an astronomical symbol. ♇

Plutonium: a transuranic radio-active element. (Pu)

Poet: a symbol used to indicate poet in directories, in which composition space and time must be saved.

Pointer: see Arrow; Index[1]; Pen dash.

Points: three dots denoting omission; also known as ellipsis or suspension points.

. . .

Polish Accents: those used in the Polish language.

ąćęłńóśźż ĄĆĘŁŃÓŚŹŻ

Polish A, E, L, Z: see Polish Accents.

Polonium: a radio-active element. (Po)

Portuguese Accents: those used in the Portuguese language.

àáâãçèéêìíòóôõúû

ÀÁÂÃÇÈÉÊÌÍÒÓÔÕÚÛ

Portuguese A, O: see Portuguese Accents.

Positive: a mathematical or electrical symbol. +

Poster Type: that made, generally of wood, in large sizes, for use in poster and similar work; its body is measured in 'lines' of 12 pt., from 4 lines upward.

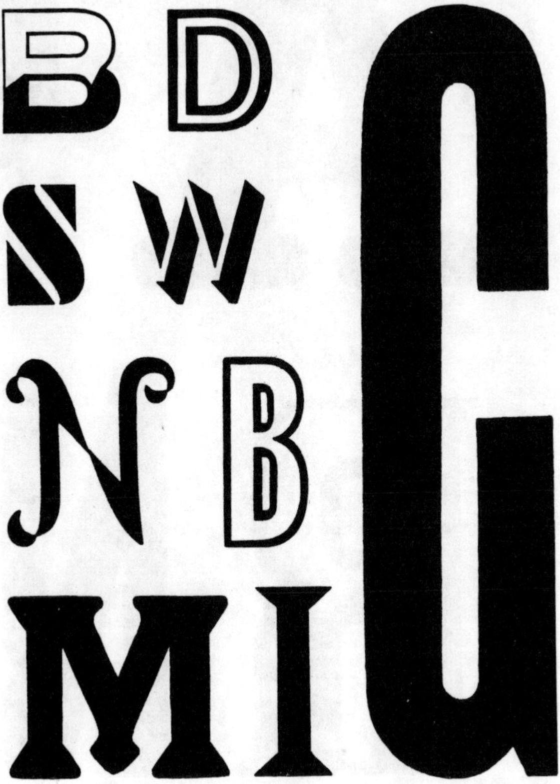

st t

A

R N

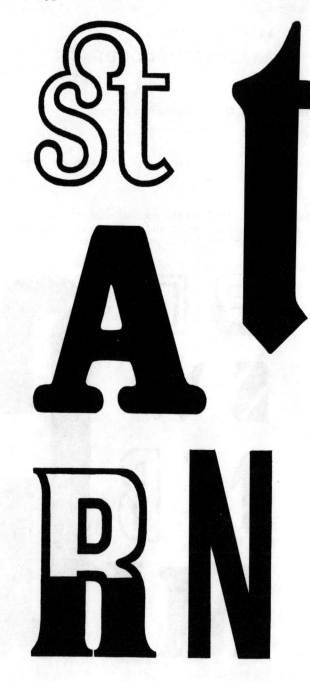

g E
2 9

TL

M

K

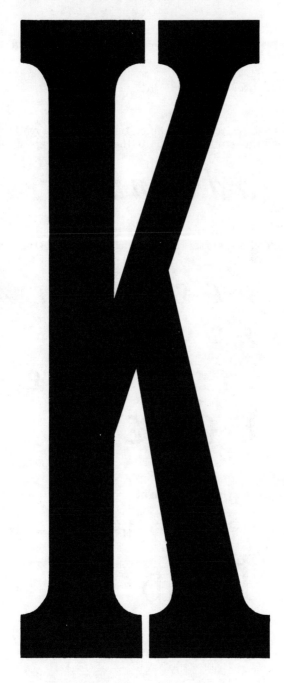

Post Wagon: see Mail Coach.

Potassium: a metallic element; takes its symbol from the word Kalium.

Ⓚ

Pothook: letters resembling the shape of a pothook *l*; now generally applied to the stem endings of italic letters.

adhinu

Pound[1]**:** a symbol for English currency (the pound sterling).

£ £ £ £ £ £ £ £ £

£ £ £ £ £ £

£ £ £ £ £ £ £ £ £

£ £ £ £ £ £

Pound[2]**:** a symbol for weight (=libra).

℔ ℔ ℔ ℔ ℔ ℔ ℔

℔ ℔

Pounds Egyptian: a monetary symbol. £E

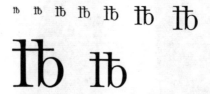

Power: see Superior figures/letters.

Praseodymium: a radio-active element. (Pr)

Product: a mathematical symbol. Π

Promethium: a rare-earth element. (Pm)

Proper Fractions: see Vulgar fractions.

Prophet: a symbol used to indicate prophet in directories, in which composition space and time must be saved.

Proportion: mathematical symbols.

$: \quad ::$

$a : b :: c : d$ reads a is to b as c is to d.

Protactinium: a radio-active element. (Pa)

Punctuation Marks: see under individual names, e.g. Comma, Hyphen, etc.

Q

Q: the seventeenth letter of the English alphabet.

Qq Qq Qq Qq

Quadrature: an astronomical situation, when one figure is at 90° from another; also known as quartile.

□

Quadrules: metal rules cast on quads of various body sizes for use in tabular composition.

— —— ——— ———— —————

Quadruple Prime: a mathematical symbol. ⁗

Quaint Characters: those formerly used, such as the long S and its various ligatures.

ſ ſb ſſ ſh ſi

Quaint Characters: CONTINUED

ſt ſk ſl ſſi ſſl

ſa ſc ſe ſh

ſi ſk ſo ſs ſu

ſſ ſſa ſſe ſſi

ſſl ſſo ſſu

Q U QU

Quartile: see Quadrature.

Quaver: a black, stemmed note in music with transverse line; half the value of the crotchet.

Queen: see Chess.

Query: see Question.

Question: a punctuation mark, indicating doubt, uncertainty, question; also called the query, or mark or note of interrogation.

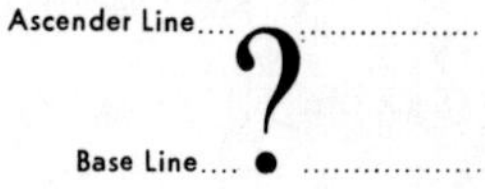

Quill: see Author.

Quintile: an astronomical aspect (72°). ⊙

Quotation Marks: inverted commas and apostrophes used to denote a quotation, extract or speech; see also Guillemets.

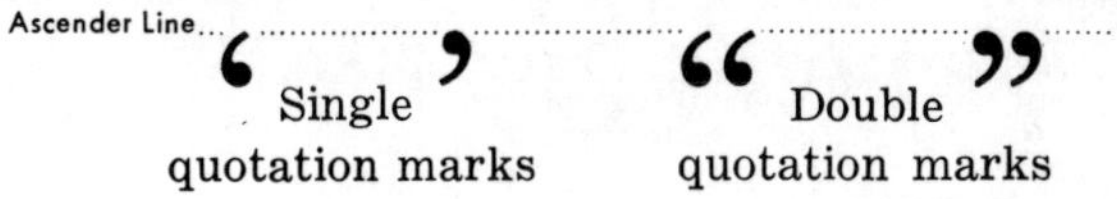

R

R: the eighteenth letter of the English alphabet.

Rr Rr *Rr* Rr

Rabbinical: see Hebrew alphabet.

Radical: see Root.

Radium: a metallic element. (Ra)

Radius: see Bracket[2].

Radix: see Root.

Radon: a gaseous element. (Rn)

Railway: a cartographical symbol. ┼┼┼┼

Rain: a meteorological symbol. ● or ●

Rainbow: a meteorological symbol. ⌒

Ratio: see Proportion.

Recipe: a medical symbol.

℞ ℞ ℞ ℞

℞ ℞ ℞ ℞ ℞ ℞

Rectangle: a geometrical sign. ▭

Reference Marks: those used in bookwork; see Asterisk, Dagger, Double Dagger, Section, Parallel, Paragraph.

Registration Sign: a symbol used to indicate proprietorship legally protected, as in Registered trade mark.

® ® ® ® ® ® ®

Reis: a symbol used in South American currencies.

Religious Signs: see under individual names, e.g. Crowned M, etc.

Renaissance Border: one consisting of grouped lines and shell-like motif.

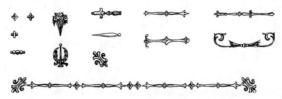

Renaissance Border: CONTINUED

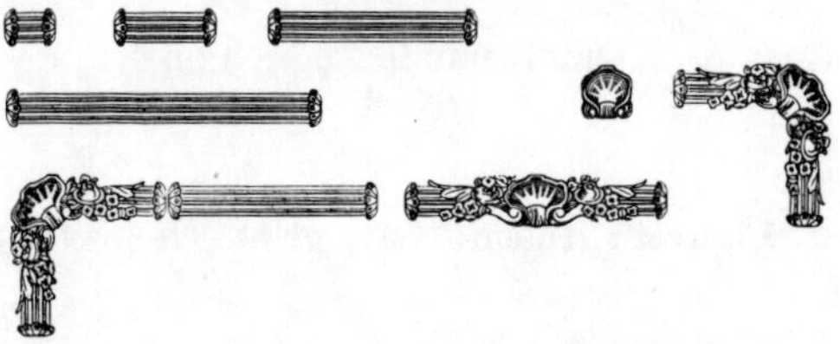

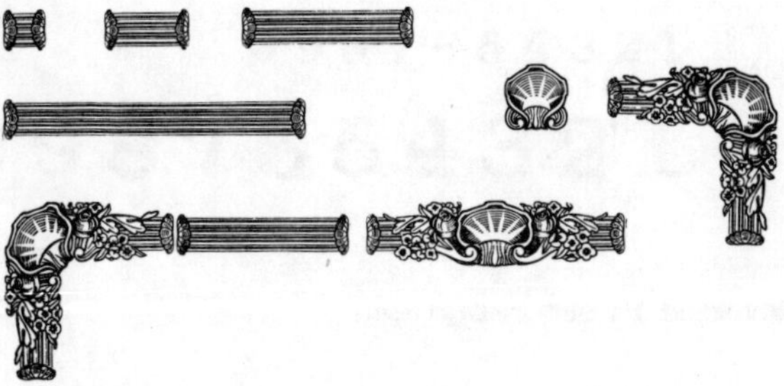

Repeat: a symbol used in music indicating repetition of part of the composition.

 or 

Repetition: see Nuller.

Resch: see Hebrew alphabet.

Response: an ecclesiastical symbol. ℟ ℟ ℟ ℟

Rest: symbols used to denote cessation of sound in music.

semibreve mimim

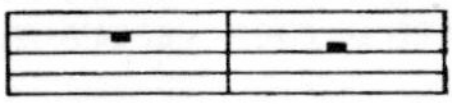

crotchet quaver semi-quaver demisemi-quaver

Reversed Cedilla: a turned form of cedilla, appearing on several consonants in a variety of languages, as in

Ewe ḑ Old Icelandic ǫ Polish ą ę

Reversed Figures: those that print the wrong way round.

Reversed P: see Paragraph.

Reversed Prime: a mathematical symbol. ‵

Reversed Type[1]: that that prints the wrong way round.

 Record Gothic Offset

Reversed Type[2]: see Cameo.

Reversible Reaction: a chemical reaction proceeding in either direction. ⇌

Rhenium: a metallic element. (Re)

Rhizocarp: a plant with stem that dies yearly but with perennial root. 

Rho: see Greek alphabet.

Rhodium: a metallic element. 

Rhombus: a geometrical symbol. 

Right Angle: mathematical symbols of various significance; see also Acute Angle.

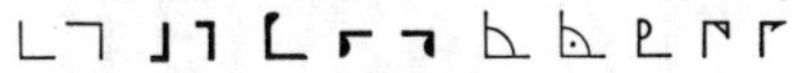

Rime: see Frost.

Rimmed: type having a fine line round the character.

Astoria

Ringed Figures/Letters: those placed within a circle.

❶ ② ❸ ④ ⑤ ⑥ ❼ ⑧ ⑨ ⓪

❶ ❷ ❸ ❹ ❺ ❻ ❼ ❽ ❾ ⓪

❶❷❸❹❺❻❼❽

❾⓪

① ② ③ ④ ⑤ ⑥ ⑦ ⑧ ⑨ ⓪

❶ ❷ ❸ ❹ ❺ ❻ ❼ ❽ ❾ ⓪

①②③④⑤⑥⑦⑧⑨⓪

❶❷❸❹❺❻❼❽❾⓪

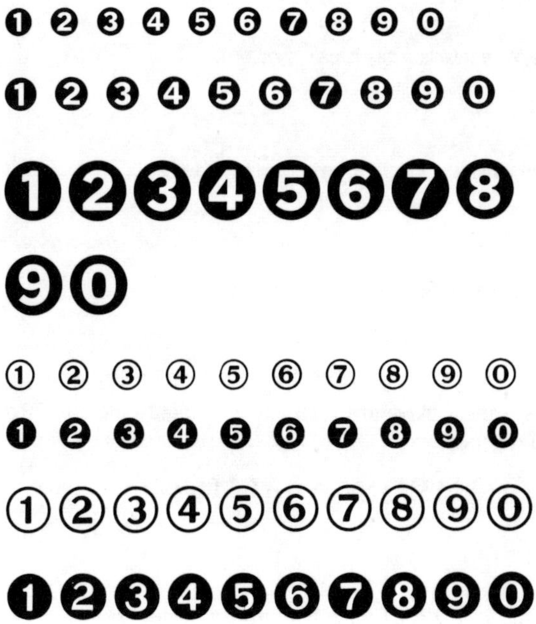

Ringed Figures/Letters: CONTINUED

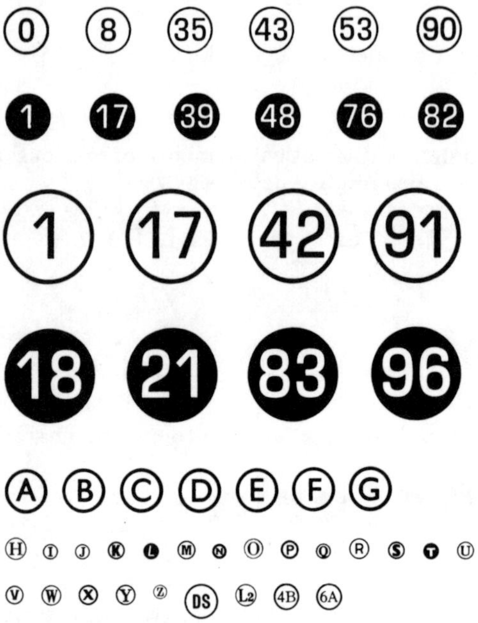

Road: a cartographical symbol. ═

Roman: see Latin characters; Upright.

Roman Cross: see Latin cross.

Romanian Accents: those as used in the Romanian language.

àâăèìîşţù ÀÂĂÈÌÎŞŢÙ

Romanian A, S, T: see Romanian Accents.

Roman Numerals: those numerating by the use of letters of the alphabet.

I=1	II=2	V=5	X=10
L=50	C=100	M=1000 etc.	

Ronde: a flowing letter, of script design: (a) upright, (b) inclined.

(a) Parisian Ronde

(b) *Madonna Ronde*

Rook: see Chess.

Root: a mathematical symbol, known also as radical or radix (see also Cube root, Square root).

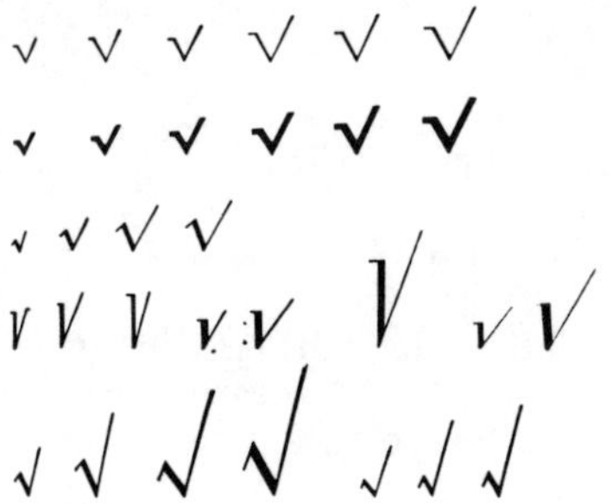

Round A: see Commercial A.

Round And: see Ampersand.

Round Brackets: see Parenthesis.

Round Sorts: those designed as circles or arcs of circles, or in which these exert a strong influence on the letter form.

c e o D G Q

Royal Arms: the heraldic device of the Crown.

Rubidium: a metallic element. (Rb)

Rule: printing material, made of brass, zinc, type metal, steel, wood, etc., used for decorative or bordering purposes; plain or patterned face.

Rule: CONTINUED

Rule: CONTINUED

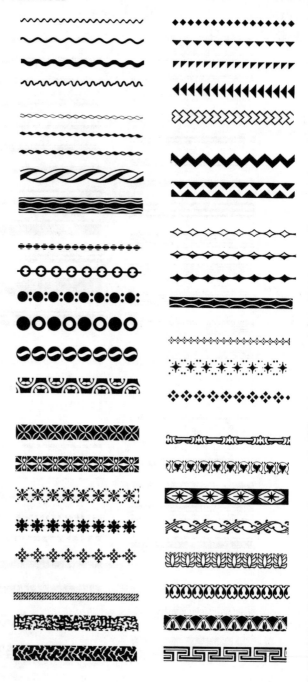

Ruled: a type face composed or with a background of lines.

PRISMA

GILL SANS

CAMEO

RULED

Runic Cross: see Celtic cross.

Rupee: a symbol used in Indian currency.

singular ~~R~~ plural ~~Rs~~ Lakhs of rupees ~~Rx~~

Russian: the language of Russia; the alphabet consists of 31 symbols, based on the Cyrillic alphabet modified from the Greek and introduced by St. Cyril in the ninth century.

абвгдежзийклмнопрстуфхцчшщъыьэюя
АБВГДЕЖЗИЙКЛМНОПРСТУФХЦЧШ
ЩЪЫЬЭЮЯ

абвгдежзийклмнопрстуфхцчшщъыьэюя
АБВГДЕЖЗИЙКЛМНОПРСТУФХЦЧ
ШЩЪЫЬЭЮЯ

Russian: CONTINUED

абвгдежзийклмнопрстуфхцчшщъыьэюя
АБВГДЕЖЗИЙКЛМНОПРСТУФХЦЧШЩ
ЪЫЬЭЮЯ

абвгдежзийклмнопрстуфхцчшщъыьэюя
АБВГДЕЖЗИЙКЛМНОПРСТУФХЦЧШЩ
ЪЫЬЭЮЯ

абвгдежзийклмнопрстуфхцчшщъыьэюя
АБВГДЕЖЗИЙКЛМНОПРСТУФХЦЧШЩ
ЪЫЬЭЮЯ

абвгдежзийклмнопрстуфхцчшщъыьэюя
АБВГДЕЖЗИЙКЛМНОПРСТУФХЦЧШЩЪЫЬЭЮЯ

абвгдежзийклмнопрстуфхцчшщъыьэюя
АБВГДЕЖЗИЙКЛМНОПРСТУФХЦЧШ
ЩЪЫЬЭЮЯ

Russian Accent: the short accent. ˘ (Й)

Ruthenium: a metallic element. (Ru)

S

S: the nineteenth letter of the English alphabet.

𝕾𝖘 Ss 𝒮𝓈 Ss

Sacred Heart (and Crown): an ecclesiastical symbol.

Sagittarius: see Zodiac, Signs of.

St. Andrew's Cross: a cross in the form of the letter X; also known as crux decussata or saltire cross; the same form is used for St. Patrick's cross.

X

St. Anthony's Cross: an ecclesiastical symbol in the form of the Greek letter tau (T); also known as crux commissa; egyptian; patibulata; tau cross.

T

St. George's Cross: a cross similar in design to the Greek cross (q.v.).

St. Patrick's Cross: see St. Andrew's cross.

Saltire Cross: see St. Andrew's cross.

Samarium: a rare-earth element. (Sm)

Samech: see Hebrew alphabet.

Sandstorm: a meteorological symbol. 

Sanserif: a design of type without stem terminations (sans = without; serif = a line or termination); also called Block letter.

Advertisers Gothic Condensed

Annonce Grotesque

BASUTO

BELL GOTHIC BOLD

Bernhard Gothic Extra Heavy

Binder-Style

Braggadocio

BRITANNIC

BROADWAY

CONDENSED SANS SERIFS No. 5

CONDENSED TITLE GOTHIC NO. 11

EMPIRE

Eurostile

FOLIO LIGHT

Franklin Gothic Wide

Futura Display

GILL SANS TITLING

GRANBY

GROTESQUE No. 8

Helvetica

IMPACT

Information

Inserat Grotesk

MICROGRAMMA

MODERNIQUE

PEIGNOT Bold

Radiant Heavy

Record Gothic Condensed

Standard Extended

Topic Medium

UNIVERS Medium Condensed

Venus Bold

VOGUE

Saturn: an astronomical symbol. ♄

Scale: the relationship of height to thickness in a letter, here 6:1.

Scandinavian A: see Swedish A.

Scandinavian O: see Danish O.

Scandium: a metallic element. (Sc)

Schelling: a currency sign. 

Schwabacher: a round and free form of German black letter.

Nürnberger Schwabacher

abcdefghij

klmnopqrſs

tuvwxyz

Schwabacher: CONTINUED

Scorpio: see Zodiac, Signs of.

Scratch: the line between the numerator and denominator in fractions, especially in split fractions.

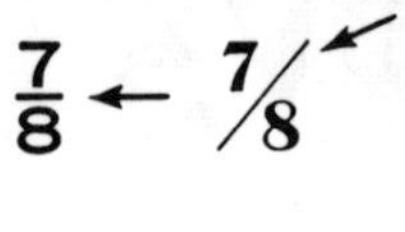

Scratch Comma: a short diagonal line used as a comma in some founts, particularly sanserifs.

Scratched Figures: also known as Cancelled (q.v.), Crossed, or Erased figures.

Screamer: see Exclamation.

Scribal Abbreviations: those used by manuscript writers; particularly single letters marked to indicate double letters.

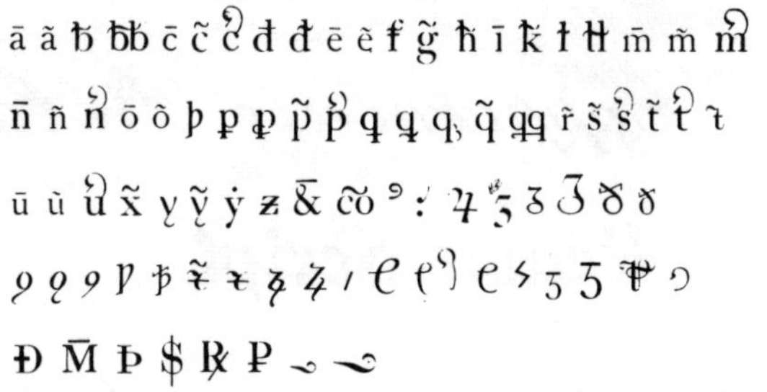

Script: type designed originally in imitation of handwriting (copperplate or otherwise), now obtainable in various display forms; script letters may appear to be joined or separate.

Amazone

Ashley Script

Bauer Brush Script

Bon Aire

Script: CONTINUED

Boulevard

Cantate

Champion

Charcoal

Charme Bold

Copperplate Bold

Heavy Script

Invitation Script

Juliet Script

Kaufmann Script

Marina Script

Mistral

Palace Script

Palette

Parkway Script

Primadonna

Reiner Script Repro Script

Slogan Stop

Swing Bold

Thompson Quillscript

Trafton Script

Virtuosa II

Waverley

Youthline Script

Scroll: a device used between cheque and counterfoil, etc.

Scruple: a medical symbol. ℈

Sculptor: a symbol used to indicate sculptor in directories, in which composition space and time must be saved.

Seal: the place on a legal document for attesting.

Second: a mathematical symbol, etc. ″

Section: the fourth bookwork reference mark; also used as symbol for the word 'Section' in book headings.

§ § § § § § §

§ § § § § §

§ § § § § §

§ § § § § § §

§ § § § § §

Sectional Brace/Bracket: see Brace; Bracket.

Sector: a mathematical symbol. ∇

Segment: a mathematical symbol. ⌓

Segol: see Masoretic points.

Selenium: a non-metallic element. (Se)

Self-Aligning Type: see Interchangeable.

Self-Spacing Type: founts of type containing certain letters cast to two different widths so that the narrow ones may be inserted if the word is too long for the measure, or vice versa.

RAINED — normal

R*AIN*ED — *narrow

Semaphore: symbols used to designate the flag positions taken by the signaller when using the semaphore system.

Semibreve: a white note in music, one-half the value of the breve.

Semicircle: a geometrical symbol. (

Semi-Colon: a punctuation point.

Semi-Quaver: a black, stemmed note in music with two lines on the stem, one-half the value of a quaver.

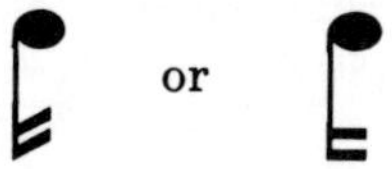

Separatrix: a dividing line; also known as the commercial stroke, diagonal, oblique, shilling stroke or solidus.

long / short (display) /

Series: the range of sizes of a particular type face.

A 6 point
A 8 point
A 10 point
A 12 point
A 14 point
A 18 point
A 24 point
A 30 point
A 36 point
A 42 point
A 48 point
A 60 point
A 72 point

Serif: the termination added to the main stems of letters.

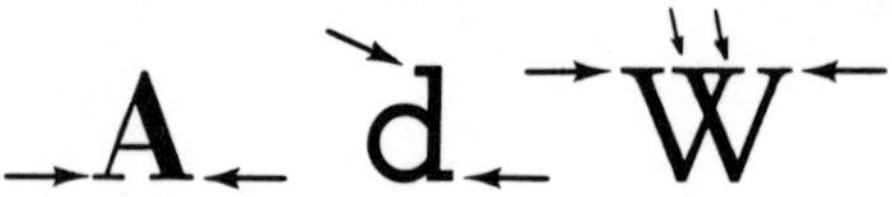

Set: the width of the type body, with which the appearance of the face is closely connected.

Seven: the symbol for a heptuple quantity.

Sextile: an astronomical aspect (60°). ⚹

Shaded[1]: where the body of the letter is indicated by faint parallel lines, vertical, diagonal or horizontal.

Adstyle Shaded

Antique Shaded

Bodoni Shaded

Cheltenham Bold Shaded

ENGRAVERS ROMAN SHADED

SPARTAN SHADED

WINCHESTER BOLD SHADED

Shaded[2]: where a white line relieves a bold type; akin to Inline.

ELONGATED ROMAN SHADED

FIGGINS SHADED

GRAPHIQUE

SANS SERIFS SHADED

Shaded Rule: that composed of lines of graduated thickness.

Shading: see Modelling.

Shadow[1]: type relieved by a thin line.

CASTELLAR

Imprint Shadow

OTHELLO SHADOW

Shadow[2]: type designed three-dimensionally to give the effect of cast shadow.

GILL SANS SHADOW 406

ROCKWELL

SHADOW

SHADOW

Shadowline: a design of type partly or wholly surrounded by a thin line.

GILL SANS SHADOW LINE

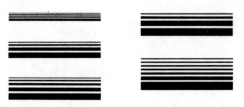

Shamrock: see Trefoil.

Shapes: patterns of various kinds, made in brass, etc., hollowed to allow of the insertion of type matter.

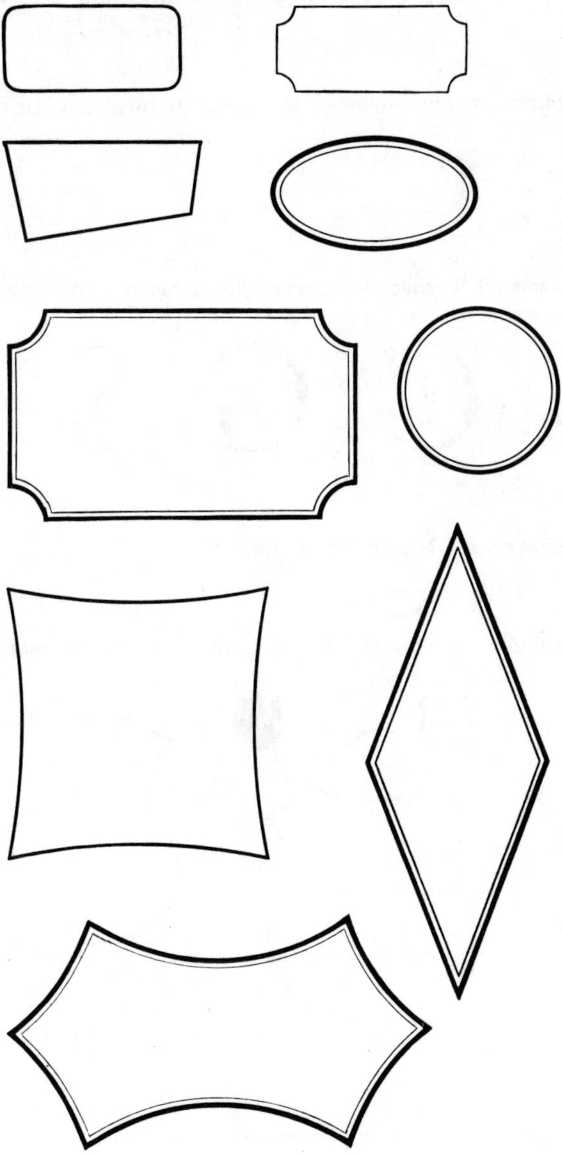

Share List Fractions: those cast on a uniform width of body, to allow of trouble-free adjustment of stock exchange quotations.

$^{1}{}_{8}$ $^{1}{}_{4}$ $^{3}{}_{8}$ $^{1}{}_{2}$ $^{5}{}_{8}$ $^{3}{}_{4}$ $^{7}{}_{8}$ $^{1}{}_{3}$ $^{2}{}_{3}$ $^{1}{}_{6}$ $^{1}{}_{16}$ $^{3}{}_{16}$ $^{5}{}_{16}$ $^{7}{}_{16}$ $^{9}{}_{16}$ $^{11}{}_{16}$ $^{13}{}_{16}$ $^{15}{}_{16}$

$^{1}{}_{32}$ $^{3}{}_{32}$ $^{5}{}_{32}$ $^{7}{}_{32}$ $^{9}{}_{32}$ $^{11}{}_{32}$ $^{13}{}_{32}$ $^{15}{}_{32}$ $^{17}{}_{32}$ $^{19}{}_{32}$ $^{21}{}_{32}$ $^{23}{}_{32}$ $^{25}{}_{32}$ $^{27}{}_{32}$ $^{29}{}_{32}$ $^{31}{}_{32}$

$^{1}{}_{8}$ $^{1}{}_{4}$ $^{3}{}_{8}$ $^{1}{}_{2}$ $^{5}{}_{8}$ $^{3}{}_{4}$ $^{7}{}_{8}$ $^{1}{}_{16}$ $^{3}{}_{16}$ $^{5}{}_{16}$ $^{7}{}_{16}$ $^{9}{}_{16}$ $^{11}{}_{16}$ $^{13}{}_{16}$ $^{15}{}_{16}$

Sharp: a symbol used in music to raise a note a semitone.

♯

Sheared Terminals: curved lines broken by serif, stem, etc.

C G S

Sheva: see Masoretic points.

Shield: an armorial bearing, designed in various forms.

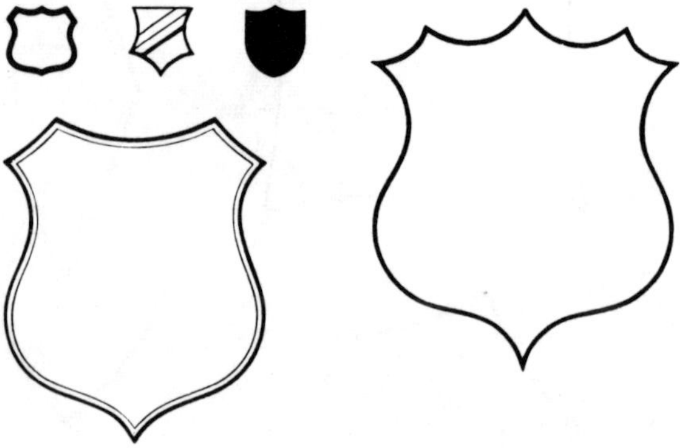

Shilling Stroke: see Separatrix.

Shin: see Hebrew alphabet.

Ship: a conventional sign for a sailing ship; see also Steamer.

Short A: see Commercial A.

Short Accent: a semi-circular line placed over a letter; also called the Breve[2].

ă ĕ ĭ ŏ ŭ

Short And: see Ampersand.

Short Ascenders: those smaller than usual on type faces.

b d f h k l

Short Descenders: those barely extruding below the base line.

j p q y

Shorthand: type made for the printing of matter in shorthand.

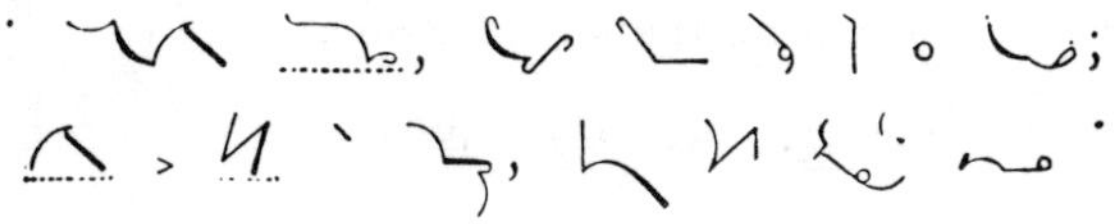

Short Letters: those occupying the centre of the body and having no ascending or descending strokes.

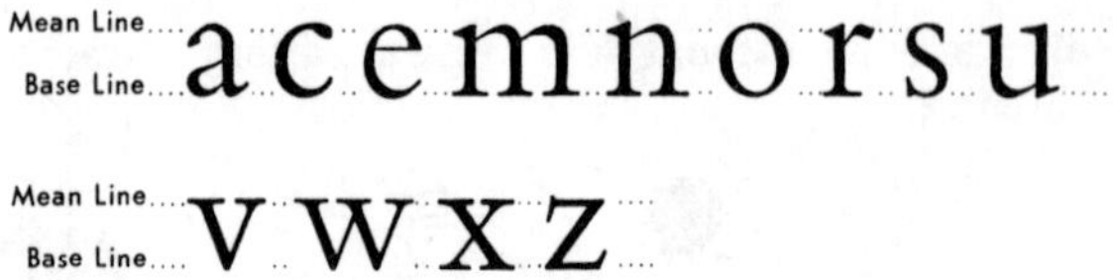

Shower: meteorological symbols of various kinds.

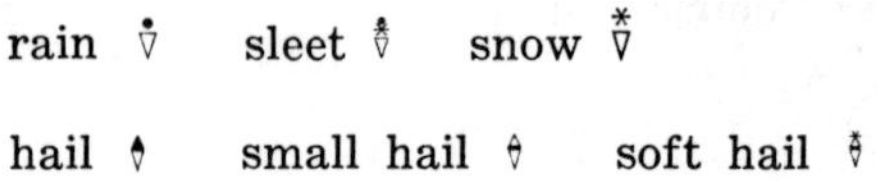

Shrub: see Frutex.

Shurek: see Masoretic points.

Sigma: see Greek alphabet.

Sign[1]**:** a miscellaneous typographical character.

a/c × √ ℔ ~ £ etc.

Sign[2]**:** a symbol in music indicating a return to a stated place.

𝄋

Signature: the symbol at the beginning of the musical stave indicating the key or time.

key 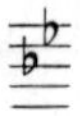 time 

Silicon: a non-metallic element. (Si)

Silver: a metallic element; takes its symbol from the Latin word Argentum.

(Ag)

Similar To: a mathematical symbol. ∽

Simplex Rule: see Milled rule.

Sin: see Hebrew alphabet.

Single Quotation Marks: see Quotation marks.

Six: the symbol for a sextuple quantity.

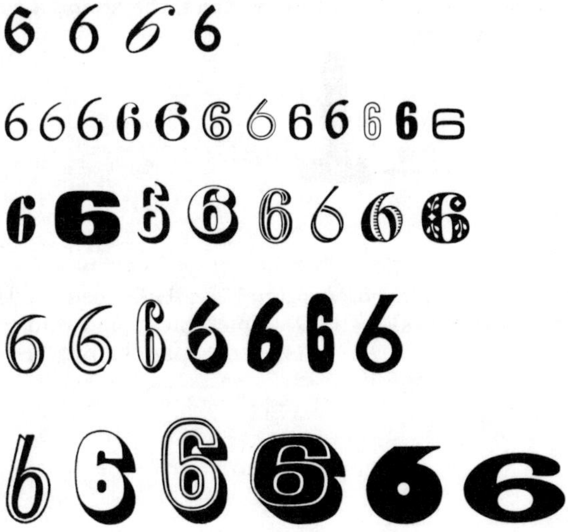

Skeleton: a very thin-line type face.

Futura Fineline

HUXLEY VERTICAL

Record Gothic

Thinline Condensed

Sky: a meteorological symbol.

clear ○ obscured ⊗

cloud 2/8 4/8 6/8 8/8

Slab Serif: a block serif, square in section, often as thick as, sometimes thicker than, the stem; also known as Flat serif.

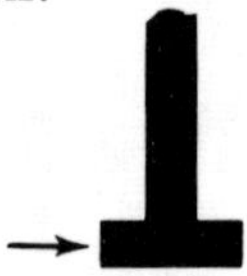

Sleeping Car: a conventional symbol, used particularly in continental railway timetables, and indicating a coach with fitted beds, etc.; also known as Schlafwagen; Wagon-lit.

Sleet: see Shower.

Sloped Roman: leaning type modelled directly on, and bearing close visual likeness to, its companion upright letter.

sloped roman

abcdefghijklmnopqrstuvwxyz

roman

abcdefghijklmnopqrstuvwxyz

Sloping Bar: an inclined bar, especially in black letter and Venetian designs.

Sloping Fractions: see Diagonal fractions.

Sloping M: that the sides of which are sloping instead of perpendicular; also called Splayed.

M M M

Sloping Type: see Italic; Script; Sloped Roman.

Slovak C, D, L, N, R, S, T, U, Z: see Slovakian Accents.

Slovakian Accents: those used in the Slovakian language.

á ä č ď é í ĺ ľ ň ó ô ŕ ř š ť ú ů ý ž

Á Ä Č Ď É Í Ĺ Ľ Ň Ó Ô Ŕ Ř Š Ť Ú Ů Ý Ž

Slur[1]**:** the terminals at the end of certain strokes, etc., in old face types.

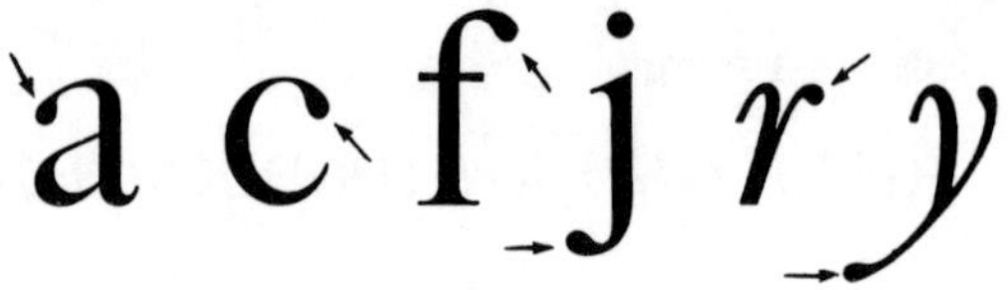

Slur[2]**:** a symbol used in music to connect notes to be played in a smooth manner (see also Bind).

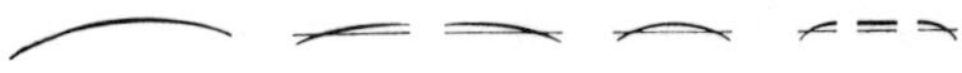

Slur Serif: that of bulbous shape, as in Cooper (see also Concave serif).

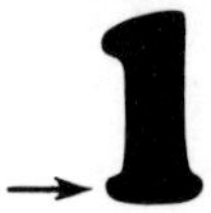

Small Capitals: a size of letter of uniform height, reduced facsimiles of capitals.

lower-case	small capitals	capitals
abcdefghij	ABCDEFGHIJ	ABCDEFGHIJ
klmnopqr	KLMNOPQR	KLMNOPQR
stuvwxyz	STUVWXYZ	STUVWXYZ

Small Face: a type cast on a body larger than necessary or normal.

Smoke: see Haze.

Snow: meteorological symbols varying according to the state or condition of the snow: 

lying drift (high) drift (low) granular

Snowstorm: a meteorological symbol. 

Sodium: a metallic element; takes its symbol from the chemists' Latin word Natrium.

Solar: see Corona[1].

Solid Fractions: those made in one piece, in contradistinction to split fractions; also known as Whole fractions.

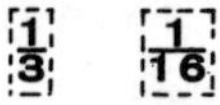

Solidus: see Separatrix.

Sort: the unit of a fount, i.e. the single letter or stamp.

a or **b** or **N** or **3** or **?** etc.

Sou: a unit of French currency. 

Space: a typographical symbol. #

Space Notes: those in music placed between lines. 

Spade: see Card pips.

Spanish Accents: the acute, diaeresis and tilde are used.

áéíñóúü ÁÉÍÑÓÚÜ

Spanish N: see Spanish Accents; Tilde.

Speisewagen: see Dining car.

Spherical Angle: a geometrical symbol. ∢

Spine: the main stem of the letter S.

Splayed M: see Sloping M.

Split Fractions: sets of figures in which the numerator and denominator are separate types; the dividing stroke is usually cast on the lower section; cast to half the depth of body with which they are used; may be combined to give any fraction.

1 2 3 4 5 6 7 8 9 0 ‾1 2 3 4 5 6 7 8 9 0‾ 1 ‾8‾ $\frac{1}{8}$

Sport Signs: those representing various sports, such as

Spot: a black solid circle or dot used for display purposes.

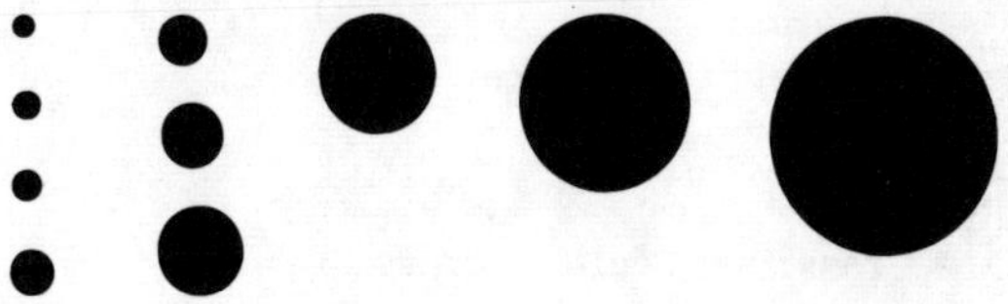

Spray: a flower ornament used as a terminal, etc.

Spur: sharp points at the reverse ends of some serifs, as on capital T.

Squalls: a meteorological symbol. ∀

Square[1]: a solid or outline display ornament.

Square[2]**:** a mathematical symbol. □

Square Bracket: see Bracket.[1]

Square Cross: see Maltese cross.

Square Root: a mathematical symbol to indicate the product of a number multiplied by itself.

√

Square Sorts: those in which the main features are straight lines or square or rectangular shapes.

H M W X Z

Squealer: see Exclamation.

Staccato: a symbol (a dot) used in music to indicate separate notes.

Staff: see Stave.

Stamps: see Type.

Standard Fount: one in which the lower-case alphabet measures 13 ems of its own body, the capitals being designed to proportionate width.

□□□□□□□□□□□□□ 10 point

abcdefghijklmnopqrstuvwxyz

Standard Letters: those used by the punch-cutter as guides to height, width and alignment.

HO mop

Star: an advertising or decorative symbol (usually distinguished from the Asterisk, q.v.).

Star: CONTINUED

Star of David: a Hebrew religious symbol. 

Statue: a symbol used to indicate statue in directories, in which composition space and time must be saved.

Stave: the set of lines and spaces used for the positioning of notes in music; also known as the staff.

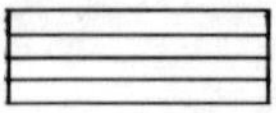

Steamer: a conventional symbol for a steamship, especially in regard to such connection with rail or road transport in timetables; see also Ship.

Stem: the main stroke of a letter.

Stencil: a type designed in imitation or suggestive of stencilled lettering.

Futura Black

Stagg

STENCIL TEA CHEST

Stereo: a special symbol to indicate richer sound in music (stereophonic). Ⓢ

Stipple: see Half-Tone.

Straight Accent: see Long accent.

Straight Commas: those similar in shape to the seconds mark; often used for digiting (see also Scratch comma).

"

Straight Fractions: those with a horizontal line between the numerator and denominator; usually an en quad wide; also known as en quad, nut quad, or two-figure fractions.

$\frac{1}{4}$ $\frac{1}{2}$ $\frac{3}{4}$ $\frac{1}{4}$ $\frac{1}{2}$ $\frac{3}{4}$

$\frac{1}{4}$ $\frac{1}{2}$ $\frac{3}{4}$ $\frac{1}{3}$ $\frac{2}{3}$ $\frac{1}{6}$ $\frac{1}{8}$ $\frac{3}{8}$ $\frac{3}{4}$

Straight of the Bowl: the straight part to which the bowl of a letter is joined.

Straits Dollar: a monetary symbol. $

Stress: see Modelling.

Strip Borders: see Continuous Borders.

Stroke, Main: see Stem.

Strontium: a metallic element. (Sr)

Stub: descriptive of a short or rounded serif.

Sub-Factorial: an expression of mathematical notation, e.g.

$\underline{n|}$ or n¡

Subtraction: see Minus.

Suffix: see Inferior figures/letters.

Suffrutex: an undershrub. ♄

Sulphur: a non-metallic element. Ⓢ

Sum: a mathematical symbol (the Greek capital sigma).

Σ

Summation Rules: a pair of thin and thick horizontal rules used below the total of figures.

Sun: an astronomical symbol. ⊙ 

Superior Figures/Letters: those cast to a size about one-half the depth of the body and positioned at the top of the shoulder; known also (in algebra) as exponents, indices, or powers; also known as Cock-up figures/letters.

H^{1234567890}

H^{abcdefghijklmnopqrstuvwxyz}

H^{ABCDEFGHIJKLMNOPQRSTUVWXYZ}

Surgeon: a symbol used to indicate surgeon in directories, in which composition space and time must be saved.

Suspension Points: see Points.

Swash: decorative alternative characters, found in some italic founts; dating from the 17th century.

A B C D E G J M N P R T V

A B C D E G L M N P R T Y &

Swash: CONTINUED

ABCDEGHJK
MNPRTUYQ

ABDEJMNRSTZ

ABCDEMPRTU

ABCDGMNPT

A B D E F M N
P R T Y

A E R S T

ABCDE

GJKk

MNPQ

RTUvw

Swastika: a religious symbol; also known as Buddhistic cross, Crooked cross, Fylfot or Gammadion.

male 卐 female 卍

Swedish A: the letter A surmounted by a small circle.

å

Swedish Accents: those used in the Swedish language.

åäö ÅÄÖ

Swelled Rule: one swelling from each end to the centre, also known as Fadeaway Dash.

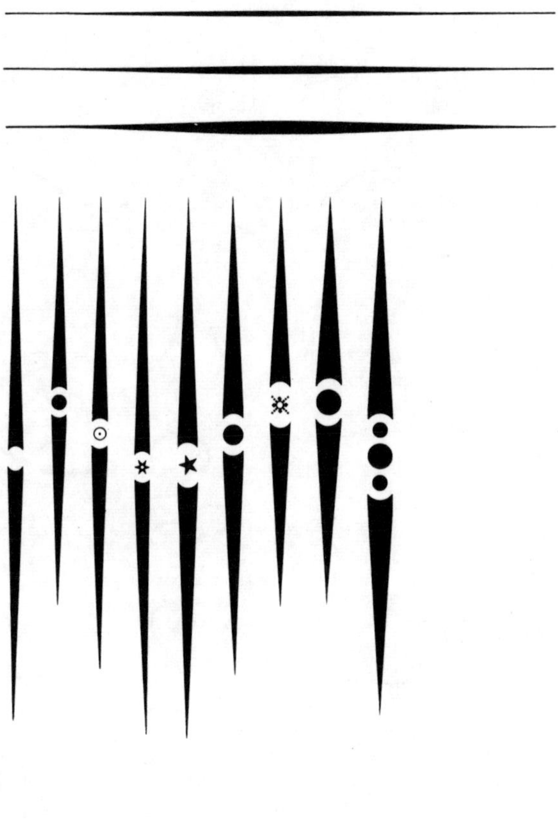

Sword: a conventional sign used to indicate knighthood, etc.; when crossed often indicates battleground in cartography.

Symbolic Signs: see under Actor, Agriculturalist, etc.

Synopsis: a list of the individual characters contained in a given fount of type, borders, ornaments, etc.

abcdefghijklmnopqrstuvwxyz
ABCDEFGHIJKLMNOPQRS
TUVWXYZ æœÆŒ ffffifl &
$£ ¶ .,-:;·!?'()/“”«»–1234567890

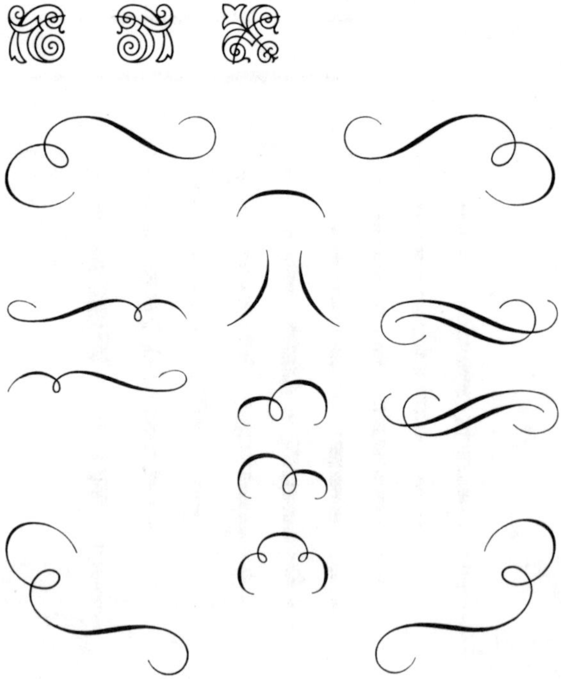

T

T: the twentieth letter of the English alphabet.

𝕿t Tt 𝒯t Tt

Tablet Border: that composed of rectangular and circular elements, open, solid or lined.

▢ ■ ▣ ○ ● ◎

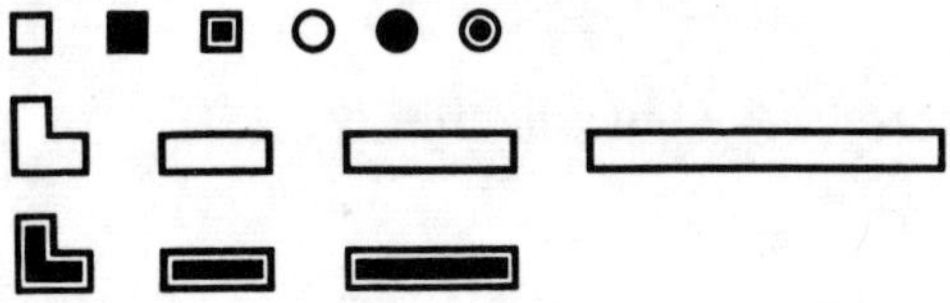

Tail: a diagonal line at the base of letters.

 k⟵ ⟶y

Tail Dot: the ball or slur at the tail of certain lower-case letters.

⟶ƒ ⟶g ⟶j ⟶y

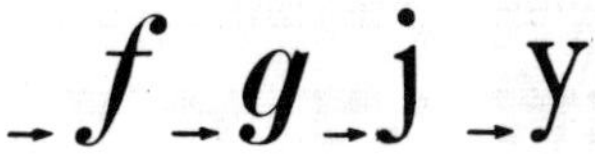

Tail Piece: an ornament used at the end of chapters, etc.

Tail Slur: see Tail Dot.

Tall Figures: see Lining figures.

Tantalum: a metallic element. (Ta)

Tartan Border: that composed of elements which, when put together, form a plaid effect.

Tau[1]**:** see Greek alphabet.

Tau[2]**:** see Hebrew alphabet.

Tau Cross: see St. Anthony's cross.

Taurus: see Zodiac, Signs of.

Tears: an ecclesiastical symbol, found in service books of the Roman Catholic Church.

Technetium: a radio-active element. (Tc)

Telegram: a conventional sign for a telegraph office, as indicated in guide books, etc.

Telephone: a conventional sign for telephone installation, as used in road books, guides, etc.

Tellurium: a non-metallic element. (Te)

Terbium: a rare-earth element. (Tb)

Terminal: the main stem of curved, non-serifed letters (see also Word terminals).

C

Terminal Letters: see Word terminals.

Teth: see Hebrew alphabet.

Tetrasporangia: a botanical symbol. ⊕

Text: see Black letter.

Thallium: a metallic element. (Tl)

Theologian: a symbol used to indicate theologian in directories, in which composition space and time must be saved.

✠

Therefore: the mathematical symbol used as a contraction for the word therefore.

∴

Theta: see Greek alphabet.

Thin Fount: one the lower-case alphabet of which measures less than 13 ems of its own body.

□□□□□□□□□□□□□ 10 point

abcdefghijklmnopqrstuvwxyz

Thirds: a mathematical sign. ‴

Thistle: the national emblem of Scotland.

Thorium: a metallic element. (Th)

Thorn: an Anglo-Saxon character, equal to th in thing (see also Eth).

þ Þ

Thousand: a commercial symbol of quantity. M

Three: the symbol for a triple quantity.

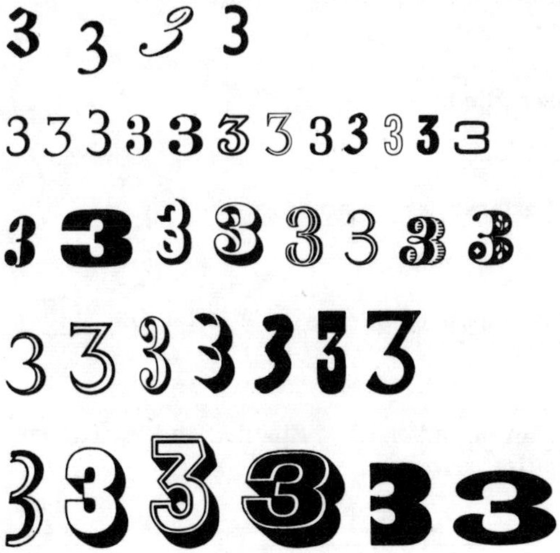

Three-Dimensional: type, etc., having the appearance of height, width and depth.

Echo NEON

PROFIL

Three-Pointed Star: a stylized form of display ornament.

Thulium: a rare-earth element. (Tm)

Thunder: a meteorological symbol. T

Thunderstorm: a meteorological symbol. ⌈↘

Tie: see Bind.

Tied Letters: see Ligatures.

Tied O: a pair of intertwining letter O.

Tilde: an accent used in Spanish and Portuguese (til) to nasalize sounds.

Spanish ñ Ñ   Portuguese ã õ Ã Õ

Tile Border: that composed of squares, outline and solid.

Tin: a metallic element; takes its symbol from the Latin word Stannum.

Sn

Tinted: a type face in which the design is made up of a dotted background.

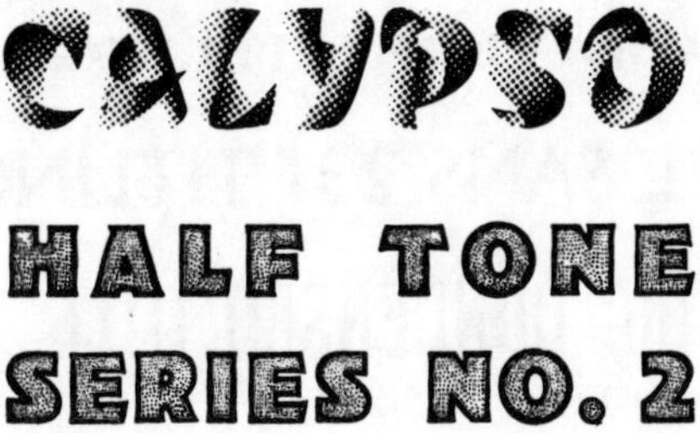

Tints: basic pattern or design motifs, commonly used as borders, tonal backgrounds, etc.

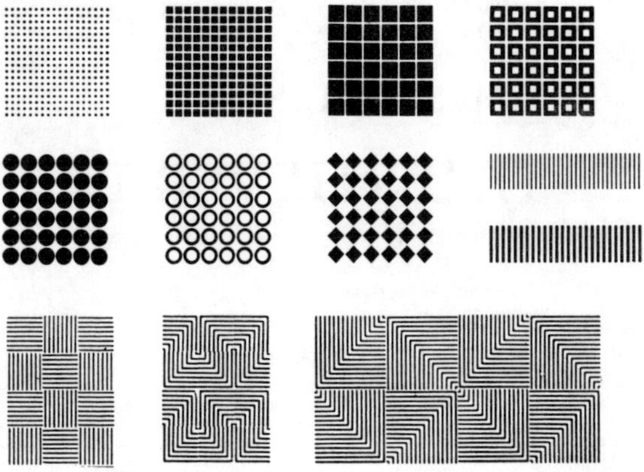

Titanium: a metallic element. Ti

Titling: capital letters, figures and punctuation points (no lower-case) cast almost to the full depth of body, thus leaving little beard.

PERPETUA type body
LIGHT TITLING

ALBERTUS TITLING

CLOISTER TITLE

ENGRAVERS TITLING

GILL SANS 231 TITLING

GOTHIC CONDENSED TITLE

GOTHIC OUTLINE TITLE

GOUDY TITLE

MICHELANGELO TITLING

TIMES TITLING

TIMES HEVER TITLING

Tones: see Tints.

Tooled: see Handtooled.

Total: see Summation rules.

Town: a cartographical symbol. ○

Trader: a symbol used to indicate trader in directories, in which composition space and time must be saved.

Train: a traditional sign for a steam locomotive.

Transitional: descriptive of type designs exhibiting traces of models preceding them, and which foreshadow later designs.

between Black letter and Venetian — The Print

between Old Face and Modern — The Print

Treble Rule: see Triple rule.

Trefoil: an ornament in the shape of a three-leaved plant; the shamrock is typical.

Trema: see Diaeresis accent.

Triangle: a mathematical sign. △

Trine: an astronomical aspect (120°). △

Triple Cross: see Papal cross.

Triple Rule: that made up of three lines of the same or different weight or pattern.

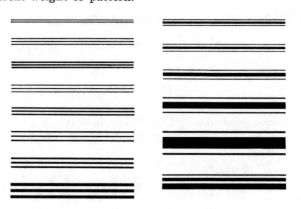

Tudor Rose: a symbolic form of rose, five petalled.

Tungsten: a metallic element; takes its symbol from the word Wolfram(ium).

Ⓦ

Turkish Accents: those used in the Turkish language, a threefold distinction being made in the i (iıî).

âçğiıîöûüş ÂÇĞİIÎÖÛÜŞ

Turkish G, I, S: see Turkish Accents.

Turn: a symbol used in music. 

Turned Commas: see Quotation marks.

Turn, Inverted: a symbol used in music. 

Two: the symbol for a double quantity.

2 2 2 2

2 2 2 2 2 2 2 2 2 2 2 2

2 2 2 2 2 2 2 2

2 2 2 2 2 2 2

2 2 2 2 2 2

Two-Colour Letters: those designed as pairs, particularly for initials; to be printed in different colours.

DUO DUO

ABCDEFGHIJ
ABCDEFGHIJ

KLMNOPQRS
KLMNOPQRS

TUVWXYZ
TUVWXYZ

ABCDeFGHIJK
ABCDeFGHIJK

ABCDEFGHIJ
ABCDEFGHIJ

ABCD
ABCD

Two-Figure Fractions: see Straight fractions.

Two-Line (Three-Line, etc.): a letter the depth of two (three, etc.) lines of a particular body.

IN two lines
of body size

HERE as
a three-line
initial letter

Type: the collective name for printing characters of letters, points, accents, etc.; also called stamps.

abcde *ABCDE* .,:;-!? áàâ *ÁÀÂ* 3456 £$/%

Typewriter Type: characters simulating those of the typewriting machine; made in various sizes and designs.

abcdefghijklmnopqrstuvwxyz

ABCDEFGHIJKLMNOPQRSTUVWXYZ&

1234567890£$, . : ; - ! ? ' % / "

10-pt. TYPEWRITER

Bulletin
Typewriter

IMPERIAL TYPEWRITER

New Model Remington No. 3

Oliver Printype

Oliver Typewriter

Ribbonface Typewriter

Silk Remington Typewriter

TYPEWRITER No. 2

Tzade: see Hebrew alphabet.

Tzeri: see Masoretic points.

U

U: the twenty-first letter of the English alphabet.

Uu Uu *Uu* Uu

Ultra: the extreme thickness of stroke in a type face.

GILL ULTRA BOLD

ULTRA BODONI

Umbrella Accent: see Circumflex accent.

Umlaut: see Diaeresis accent.

Unbracketed: describing types having serifs without filets.

r M H D R E

L T n K

Uncials: letter forms already well-developed by the fourth century A.D.

American Uncial   UNZIAL

LIBRA–a b c d e f g h i j k l

m n o p q r s t u v w x y z

Underlined Figures/Letters: those under which a short line appears; also known as underscored.

1234567890

abcdefghijklmnopqrstuvwxyz

ABCDEFGHIJKLMNOPQRSTUVWXYZ

Underscored Figures/Letters: see Underlined figures/letters.

Undershrub: see Suffrutex.

Unequal: see Inequality.

Unesco Copyright: an international copyright sign.

© © © ©

© © © © © © © © © © ©

Union Jack: the flag of Britain; obtainable also in two parts for printing in colours.

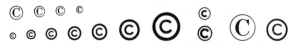

Union Jack: CONTINUED

Upper Case: another name for capitals (q.v.).

Upright: the usual forms of lettering; sometimes called roman in contradistinction to italic.

Upright or Roman *italic*

Upsilon: see Greek alphabet.

Upstroke: that made with an upward stroke of the pen, and thus normally light.

Uranium: a metallic element. (U)

Uranus: an astronomical symbol; also known as Herschel.

⛢ or ♅

Utility Rule: see Milled rule.

V

V: the twenty-second letter of the English alphabet.

𝔙𝔳 Vv *Vv* Vv

Vanadium: a metallic element. Ⓥ

Variants: alternative characters (q.v.).

Variation: a mathematical symbol. $\propto$

Vau: see Hebrew alphabet.

Vector Product: a mathematical symbol. $\wedge$

Venetian: descriptive of type faces designed in the style of pre-old face fifteenth century romans, these having fairly heavy strokes, blunt serifs, and backward stress; also known as Italian.

VERONA

abcdefghijklmnopqrstuvwxyz

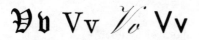

Venetian: CONTINUED

ABCDEFGHIJKLMNOPQ
RSTUVWXYZ

CENTAUR Veronese

MEDIAEVAL EUSEBIUS

Kenntonian

Venus: an astronomical symbol. ♀

Versicle: an ecclesiastical symbol.

℣ ℣ ℣ ℣ ℣

Vesta: see Asteroid.

Vibration: a symbol used in music.

$>>>$ or ∿∿∿∿∿∿∿∿∿∿

Vinculum: a horizontal line placed over figures in mathematics to connect them; also known as Bond or Brace.

——— $\sqrt{t(t-4\varepsilon^2)}$

Vine Border: that designed as vine leaves and grapes.

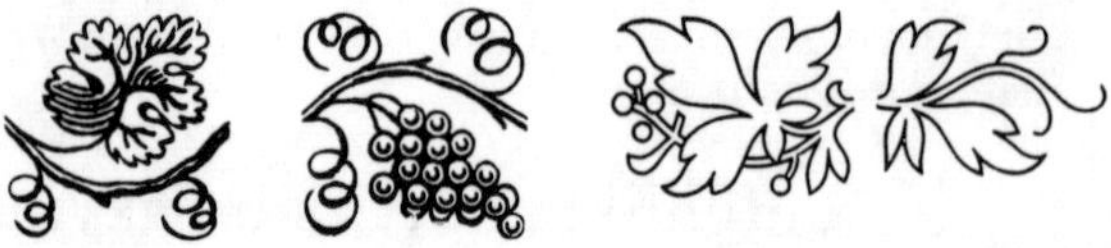

Virgo: see Zodiac, Signs of.

Voting Signs: see Ballot Paper Signs.

Vowel Points: see Hebrew alphabet.

Vowels: letters representing speech sounds.

aeiou AEIOU

Vulgar Fractions: those in which the numerator is smaller than the denominator; also known as common or proper fractions.

$\frac{1}{2}$ $\frac{9}{16}$ $\frac{49}{64}$

W

W: the twenty-third letter of the English alphabet.

Ww Ww *Ww* Ww

Waggon: see Wagon.

Wagon: a conventional sign, as used in timetables, etc., for a railway coach, etc.

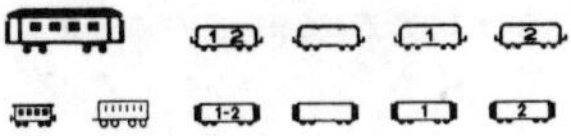

Wagon-Lit: see Sleeping car.

Wave Dash: an ornamental line or flourish.

Wavy Rule: that designed, in various weights and sizes, as an undulatory line.

Wedge Serif: a tapering serif, joining the main stem with little or no bracketing.

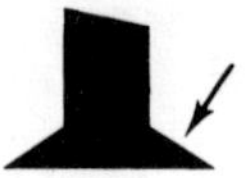

Weight: the appearance of a type face, depending on thickness of stroke, etc. (see Light, Medium, Heavy, etc.).

W E I **G H T**

Welsh Accents: those used are the circumflex, diaeresis.

äâêëîïôöûŵŷÿ ÄÂÊËÎÏÔÖÛŴŶŸ

Welsh W, Y: see Welsh Accents.

Wheel Cross: see Manx cross.

White Letter: an early name for roman types, as opposed to black letter.

ABCDEFGHIJKLMNOPQRS
TUVWXYZ
abcdefghijklmnopqrstuvwxyz

White Note: a plain note in music, as opposed to black note.

White on Black Type: see Cameo.

Whole Fractions: see Solid fractions.

Wide[1]**:** a type one remove wider than the normal.

Cheltenham Wide

Hellenic Wide

Wide Latin

Wide Sans

Wide[2]**:** see Hebrew alphabet; Self-spacing type.

Wide[3] **Fount:** one the lower-case alphabet of which measures more than 13 ems of its own body.

□□□□□□□□□□□□□ 10 point

abcdefghijklmnopqrstuvwxyz

Wing: a lateral extruder, especially on script and swash forms.

H *D* *N*

Wing Serif: that terminating an arm.

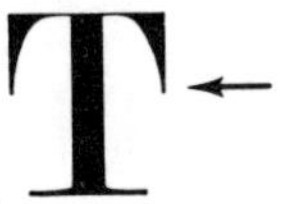

Word Terminals: ornamental or swash letters designed for use at the ends of words.

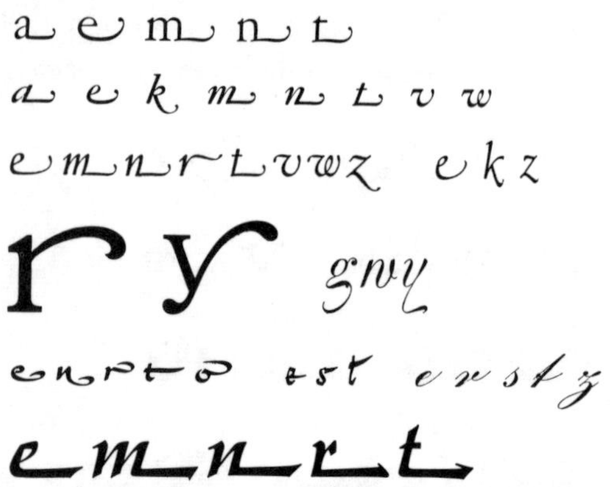

Wreath: a representation of holly, laurel, etc., in circular form.

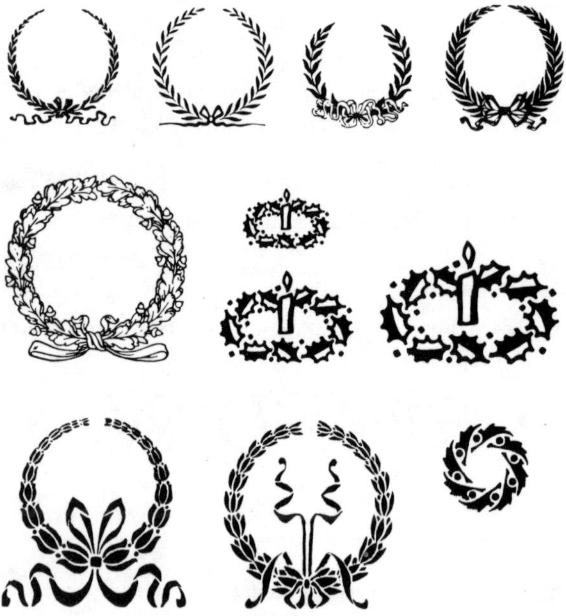

Writer: see Author.

X

X: the twenty-fourth letter of the English alphabet.

Xx Xx Xx Xx

Xenon: a gaseous element. (X)

X-Height: the height of letters of the alphabet, generally reserved to lower-case, as shown here.

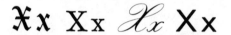

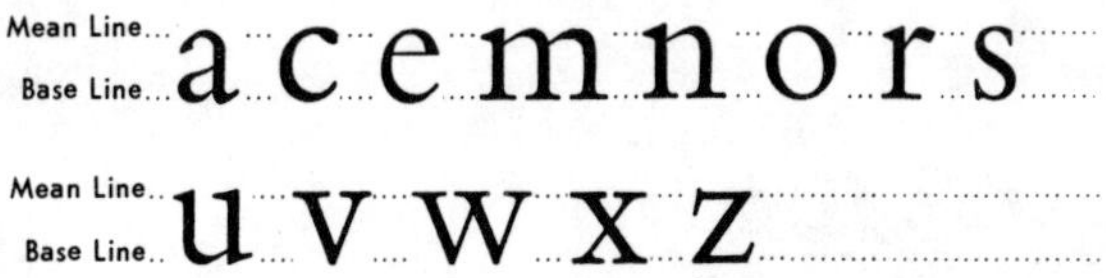

Xi: see Greek alphabet.

Xmas: see Christmas Symbols.

Y

Y: the twenty-fifth letter of the English alphabet.

Yy Yy Yy Yy

Yen: a monetary symbol (unit of Japanese currency). ¥

Yod: see Hebrew alphabet.

Ytterbium: a rare-earth element. (Yb)

Yttrium: a rare-earth element. (Y) or (Yt)

Yuletide Border: see Holly border.

Yuletide Symbols: see Christmas Symbols.

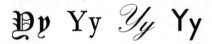

Z

Z: the twenty-sixth letter of the English alphabet.

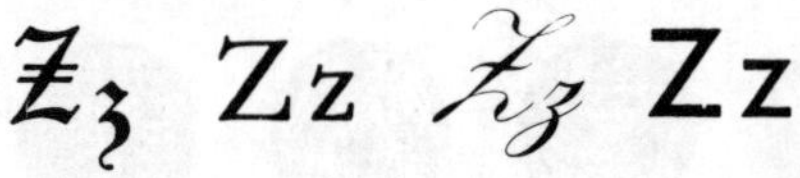

Zain: see Hebrew alphabet.

Zero: see Nullo.

Zeta: see Greek alphabet.

Zinc: a metallic element. (Zn)

Zirconium: a metallic element. (Zr)

Zodiac, Signs of: astrological symbols.

Aries (Ram)

Taurus (Bull)

Gemini (Twins)

Zodiac, Signs of: CONTINUED

Cancer (Crab)

Leo (Lion)

Virgo (Virgin)

Libra (Balance)

Scorpio (Scorpion)

Sagittarius (Archer)

Capricornus (Goat)

Aquarius (Water Carrier)

Pisces (Fishes)

Zodiacal Light: a meteorological symbol. 

GRAPHICAL GUIDE

The listing of graphic images with various names is intended to suggest directions of reference where a symbol is known but not its name. In this Guide, only some prominent feature of the symbol is shown. Its proper form appears in the Dictionary itself. Fine detail, alternative shapes, etc., are to be seen under archaeological signs, scribal abbreviations, semaphore. Also under Bulgarian, Gaelic, Glagolitic, Gothic, Greek, Hebrew, Phonetic, Pitman's Augmented, and Russian alphabets. Figures are extended in box figures, calendar, cancelled, compound fractions, dotted, electronic, erased, improper fractions, inferior, lining, old style, overlined, reversed, ringed, scratched, share list, split fractions, superior, underlined.

•	accents (floating), Braille, decimal fractions, dice, dominoes, en dot, full point, leader, Lithuanian accents, Maltese accents, Masoretic points, Polish accents, repeat, spot, staccato, Turkish accents
●	dot, moon, morse, philosopher, rain, seal, spot
:	colon, geometrical proportion, Masoretic points, proportion
··	accents (floating), Albanian accents, diaeresis, Dutch accents, Finnish accents, French accents, German accents, Icelandic accents, Masoretic points, Slovakian accents, Spanish accents, Swedish accents, Turkish accents, Welsh accents
÷	division
♟	chess
···	leader, points
∴	therefore
∵	because, Masoretic points
♣	card pips, playing cards, trefoil
·····	leader, points
::	geometrical proportion
∺	geometrical proportion
‘	breathings, Latvian accents, open quotation, quotation marks, rest
’	accents (floating), apostrophe, breathings, comma, coronis, Czech accents, drizzle, quotation marks, Slovakian accents
“	quotation marks
”	digits, quotation marks
;	semicolon
̜	reversed cedilla
°	accents (floating), Angstrom, Czech accents, degree, Finnish accents, Slovakian, Swedish a.
○	ballot paper signs, catalogue marks, circles, cotyledon, geographer, moon, picture, quintile, ringed figures, seal, shapes, sky, statue, tablet border, town
◉	county town, quintile, sun, tablet border

Φ Bulgarian, corona, farad, Greek alphabet, Russian

Θ Earth, Greek alphabet

⊕ corona, Earth, engineer, Manx cross, tetrasporangia

Ø contour integral, Danish o, double contour integral, eccentricity

⊗ ballot paper signs, cinema signs, sky

● rain, seal

☥ crux ansata

♅ Uranus

☌ conjunction, Greek alphabet

♂ male, Mars

φ philologist

⚥ hermaphrodite

♀ female, Venus

♁ Earth and Moon

☿ hermaphrodite, Mercury

♉ Zodiac signs

∝ variation

℧ commerce, prophet, tears

Ω Greek alphabet, ohm

∞ haze, infinity, monocarp, tied o

Ю Bulgarian, Russian

♋ Zodiac signs

% per cent

‰ per thousand

‱ per myriad

⬭ painter, picture

℘ sculptor, statue

☾ moon

⌓ dew, segment

☽ moon

◡ asteroid, buffet car, corona

ω archaeologist, corona, Greek alphabet

☾ moon

☽ moon

♆ Neptune

ϖ corona

⚓ officer

℈ scruple

ᵰ asteroid

⏝ aurora

⚲	asteroid
♝	chess, mitre
☛	index
⚒	blacksmith
≏	approximately equal
♂	chemist
◡	mail coach
⚘	asteroid
	zodiacal light
♕	chess, coronet
♥	card pips, catalogue marks, heart, playing cards, sacred heart
α	Greek alphabet
⚴	asteroid
♞	chess
♚	chess, coronet, crown, crowned M
❦	Brooklyn border, laurel
○	breve, draughts, grace notes, line notes, minim, music type, ovals, semibreve, shapes, space notes, white note
●	black note, composer, crotchet, demisemiquaver, draughts, grace notes, line notes, music type, quaver, semiquaver, space notes, staccato

♭	double flat, flat, signature
(	box rules, climbing, curves, parenthesis, semicircle
ˎ	accents (floating), Polish accents, reversed cedilla
⌒	arc, bind, box rules, climbing, Greek circumflex, pause, philologist, rainbow, sector, slur
)	box rules, climbing, curves, parenthesis, scruple
∪	accents (floating), box rules, Romanian accents, Russian accent, short accent, Turkish accents
≍	equivalent to
⏗	doubtful length
≬	between, mirage
♓	Zodiac signs
	apothecary
⊂	box rules, curves, implied by
∩	box rules, curves, physicist
⊃	box rules, clef, curves, implies, not contains
∪	box rules, curves, egg and dart border, musician
	laurel, poet, renaissance border, wreath
☊	curves, node, Zodiac signs,

Ч Bulgarian, Russian

℧ curves, lyre, musician, node

 actor

~ accents (floating), alternation, curves, difference between, Portuguese accents, scroll, similar to, Spanish accents, tilde, turn, turn inverted, wave dash

≃ approximately equal

≅ nearly equal to

≈ approximately equal, curves

෴ curves, frost, scroll, similar to

∼∼∼ baroque, curves

∿∿∿ vibration, wavy rule

♒ Zodiac signs

ζ Greek alphabet

 ornithologist

 entomologist

ε Greek alphabet, physician, surgeon

⌇ dust, physician, surgeon

 trader

? question

& ampersand

 clef

§ section

∫ contour integral, double contour integral, double s, integration, long s, scroll

⏞ brace, scroll

| bar, bond, graphical formula, modulus, perpendicular

‖ bond, double bars, graphical formula, nuller, parallel, straight commas

 clef

Л Bulgarian, Russian

▮▮▮ milled rule, tartan border

— accents (floating), bond, em rule, en rule, graphical formula, hyphen, Latvian accents, Lithuanian accents, long accent, Masoretic points, metal rule, minus, morse, negative, overlined figures, rest, quadrules, scratch, underlined figures, vinculum

--- canal

++++ railway

= bond, double rule, equal, fog, graphical formula, leger lines, road, summation rules

≒ approximately equal

≑ approximately equal

⫨ equilateral

≠ inequality, not equal

И Bulgarian, Russian

≡ congruence, fog, mist, non-congruence, triple rule

≡ fog, shaded rule, triple rule

Ξ Greek alphabet

≢ non-congruence, papal cross

∟ angles, factorial, right angle

⌟ angles, right angle, sub-factorial

Γ gamma function

⊥ miner, perpendicular

⊢ assertion

T geologist, Masoretic points, St. Anthony's cross, thunder

Π Greek alphabet, product, Russian, Zodiac signs

⊓ bind

] bracket, display brackets, open bracket

[bracket, display brackets, open bracket

⊔ bed, couchette, frost, sleeping car

П Bulgarian, Russian

Ш Bulgarian, Neptune, Russian

Щ Bulgarian, Russian

corner piece

卐 swastika

\+ addition, Capuchin cross, church, cross crosslet, double Jerusalem cross, Greek cross, Jerusalem cross, Maltese cross, medals, ornamental cross, positive, theologian

† dagger, decease, Latin cross, ornamental cross, Oxford corner, sword

‡ double dagger, Lorraine cross, patriarchal cross, railway

± minus or plus, plus or minus

\# equal and parallel, number, sharp, space

□ ballot paper signs, box, catalogue marks, crossword puzzle, cube, quadrature, square, tablet border, tile border

♊ Zodiac signs

☒ ballot paper signs

▣ tartan border

philatelist

▭ box, rectangle

■ castle, crossword puzzle, square, tablet border, tartan border, tile border

bed, couchette, sleeping car

automobile

customs

Brooklyn border, lectern, literary work

` accents (floating), Dutch accents, French accents, grave accent, Italian accents, Maltese accents, Portuguese accents, reversed prime, Romanian accents

\ bond, chain, graphical formula

historian

\\ bond, chain, graphical formula, inclined parallels

´ accents (floating), acute accent, Croatian accents, Czech accents, Dutch accents, foot, French accents, Icelandic accents, minute, Polish accents, Portuguese accents, scratch comma, Slovakian accents, Spanish accents

/ bond, chain, graphical formula, scratch, separatrix, surgeon

″ accents (floating), inch, second

// bond, chain, graphical formula, inclined parallels

‴ thirds

⁗ quadruple prime

author, gale

× crux decussata, dining car, double sharp, four-pointed star, geologist, hybrid, multiplication, orders, St. Andrew's cross

agriculturalist

battle, sword

* asterisk, astronomer, breath, comet, fixed star, lighthouse, naissance, philosopher, sextile, snow, star

⁂ asterism

philosopher

Ψ Greek alphabet

Ж Bulgarian, Russian

Ѫ Bulgarian

< angular bracket, arrow head, barb, crescendo, less

∧ accents (floating), Albanian accents, arrow head, barb, breath, Bulgarian, caret, chevron, circumflex, Dutch accents, Esperanto, French accents, Greek alphabet, Italian accents, Maltese accents, Portuguese accents, Romanian accents, Turkish accents, vector product, Welsh accents

λ Greek alphabet

> angular bracket, arrow head, barb, contains, decrescendo, greater than, vibration

∨	accents (floating), arrow head, barb, chevron, Croation accents, Czech accents, Esperanto, frost, inverted circumflex, Latin accents, Lithuanian accents, sector, shower, Slovakian accents, squalls, Zodiac signs
⦣	acute angles, angles, graphical formula
∠	acute angles, angles, graphical formula, spherical angle
⦤	acute angles
∠	acute angles, spherical angle
√	cube root, root, square root
∢	spherical angle
≯	not greater
≮	not less
⦤	not greater
⦥	not less
≦	less than or equal to
≧	greater than or equal to
⊻	equiangular
«	guillemets
»	guillemets
⩽	less than or equal to
⋛	greater or less
⋚	less or greater
Σ	Greek alphabet, sum
⏜	apothecary, lawyer, pharmacist
↟	Zodiac signs
←	arrow, direction
↑	arrow, direction
⇑	broad arrow, direction
⟶	approaches, arrow, direction, dust, mythologist, sandstorm
↓	arrow, direction
↯	direction, lightning
⬀	direction, thunderstorm
↔	ice, mutuality
⇄	double reversed arrow, reverse reaction
⤻	snow
↻	clockwise, direction
↺	anticlockwise, direction
△	catalogue marks, caution, differential, evergreen, finite difference, Greek alphabet, ice, increment, nabla, snow, triangle, trine
▱	rhombus

◇	asteroid, catalogue marks, diamond rule, diamonds, lozenge, playing cards, shapes, shower
⬩	black letter
◆	card pips, diamond rule, diamonds
♮	natural
⬠	pentagon
⬡	hexagon, mineralogist
❙	box rule, breath, cuneiform, dash, pen dash, separatrix, straight commas
⁊	black letter
!	exclamation, factorial, sub-factorial
♜	chess
	ermine
⚚	caduceus
★	asteroid, astronomer, comet, crux stellata, fixed star, naissance, star
♠	card pips, playing cards
	aeroplane
A	architect, Argon, cinema signs
Я	Bulgarian, Russian
@	arroba, commercial a
Ac	Actinium
℅	account
Æ	diphthong
Ag	Silver
Al	Aluminium
Am	Americium
As	Arsenic
At	Astatine
Au	Gold
B	bolivar, Boron
Б	Bulgarian, Russian
Ba	Barium
Be	Beryllium
Bi	Bismuth
Bk	Berkelium
Br	Bromine
β	Greek alphabet, phonetic alphabet
б	Bulgarian, Russian
Ь	Bulgarian, Russian
Ъ	Bulgarian, Russian
ѣ	Bulgarian
Ы	Russian

C	Carbon, Ceres, clef, Unesco copyright
¢	barred C, cent, colones
Ca	Calcium
Cd	Cadmium
Ce	Cerium
Cf	Californium
Ch	Bronze
Cl	Chlorine
Cm	Curium
c/m	centimetre
Co	Cobalt
c/o	care of
Cr	Chromium
Cr.	creditor
Cs	Caesium
Cu	Copper
D	differential
Đ	Croatian accents, eth, Icelandic D
Д	Bulgarian, Russian
đ	Croatian accents, eth, Icelandic accents
δ	dele, delta, differential, Greek alphabet
Dr.	debtor
Dy	Dysprosium
E	pounds Egyptian
ε	Greek alphabet
Er	Erbium
Eu	Europium
F	digamma function, Fluorine
f	forte
Fe	Iron
ff	fortissimo
fff	fortississimo
Fr	Francium
Γ	Bulgarian, gamma function, Greek alphabet, Russian
ℨ	minim
Ga	Gallium
Gd	Gadolinium
Ge	Germanium
H	Hydrogen
Ħ	Maltese H
♅	Uranus
♄	Saturn, Uranus

ђ caulocarp

ħ Maltese h

He Helium

Hf Hafnium

Hg Mercury

Ho Holmium

I Iodine

In Indium

Ir Iridium

K Potassium

Kr Krypton

£ cheque rule, lire, pound, pounds Egyptian

ł Polish alphabet

La Lanthanum

℔ pound

Li Lithium

LS seal

Lu Lutetium

M monaural, thousand

M̄ million

M mix

M crowned M

ℳ Mark

μ Greek alphabet, modulus

♏ minim, Zodiac signs

♍ Zodiac signs

mf mezzo-forte

Mg Magnesium

m/m millimetre

Mn Manganese

Mo Molybdenum

N Nitrogen

n sub-factorial

η Greek alphabet

ŋ Pitman's augmented alphabet

Na Sodium

Nb Niobium

Nd Neodymium

Ne Neon

Ni Nickel

Np Neptunium

O Oxygen

Ø Danish o

Θ	Greek alphabet
σ	Greek alphabet
Œ	diphthong
Os	Osmium
P	paragraph, per, peseta, peso, pfennig, Phosphorus, Pluto
p	piano
ρ	Greek alphabet
þ	Icelandic P, thorn
Þ	Icelandic, thorn
⅌	per
¶	paragraph
Pa	Protactinium
Pb	Lead
Pd	Palladium
Pf	Pfennig
♇	Pluto
Pm	Promethium
Po	Polonium
pp	pianissimo
ppp	pianississimo
Pr	Praseodymium
Pt	Platinum
Pu	Plutonium
Q	curly Q, swash
R	registration sign
Ꞧ	rupee
℞	recipe, response
Ra	Radium
Rb	Rubidium
Re	Rhenium
Rh	Rhodium
Rn	Radon
Ru	Ruthenium
S	dust, sandstorm, schelling, section, similar to, sou, stereo, Sulphur
$	dollar, reis, repeat, sign, Straits dollar
Sb	Antimony
Sc	Scandium
Se	Selenium
Si	Silicon
Sm	Samarium
Sn	Tin

Sr	Strontium
T	crux ansata, St. Anthony's cross, thunder
Ta	Tantalum
Tb	Terbium
Tc	Technetium
Te	Tellurium
Tʜ	almanack signs
Th	Thorium
Ti	Titanium
Tl	Thallium
Tm	Thulium
Tᴜ	almanack signs
U	cinema signs, Uranium
V	accents (floating), Vanadium
℣	versicle
♈	Zodiac signs
♑	Zodiac signs
ν	Greek alphabet
W	Tungsten
W̄	mordent
₩	mordent
ω	Greek alphabet, Pitman's augmented alphabet
X	cinema signs, Xenon
χ	Greek alphabet, phonetic alphabet
Y	yen, Yttrium
γ	Greek alphabet
Yb	Ytterbium
Z	rhizocarp
Zn	Zinc
Zr	Zirconium
1	annual, monocarp
2	biennial, monocarp
3	Bulgarian, Russian, scruple
ʒ	drachm
℥	ounce
♃	Jupiter, perennial
̧	accents (floating), Albanian accents, cedilla, Ceres, French accents, Greek alphabet, Lithuanian accents, Portuguese accents, Romanian accents, Turkish accents
5	arbuscula, suffrutex
5̄	arbor, frutex
0	air (pure), asteroid